Cooking with Booze

RYAN JENNINGS
& DAVID STEELE

Cooking *with* Booze

whitecap

To our mothers,
who never fed us a TV dinner in our lives.

All recommendations are made without guarantee on the part of the author or Whitecap Books Ltd. The author and publisher disclaim any liability in connection with the use of this information. For additional information, please contact Whitecap Books, 351 Lynn Avenue, North Vancouver, British Columbia, Canada V7J 2C4.

Visit our website at www.whitecap.ca.

Editor: Lesley Cameron
Proofreader: Joan Tetrault
Design & Illustrations: Five Seventeen / www.PicaPica.ca
Photography: Geoffrey Ross
Digital Artist: Jeff Mayhew
Food Styling: Ryan Jennings and David Steele
Props: HomeSense

Printed and bound in Canada

LIBRARY AND ARCHIVES CANADA CATALOGUING IN PUBLICATION

Jennings, Ryan
    Cooking with booze / Ryan Jennings, David Steele.

Includes index.

ISBN 1-55285-762-X
ISBN 978-1-55285-762-5

1. Cookery (Liquors). I. Steele, David, 1973- II. Title.

TX726.J45 2006   641.6'2   C2005-906772-1

The publisher acknowledges the financial support of the Government of Canada through the Book Publishing Industry Development Program for our publishing activities.

CONTENTS

INTRODUCTION

Cooking with Booze is about two things—eating and drinking. It applies the chutzpah of frat antics and open-bar weddings to one of the last bastions of cold sobriety—the kitchen. Much like the two of us, this book was conceived in a bar and raised in the kitchen. And, for the most part, everything seems to have turned out all right.

Over the years we've had countless ideas surface as we threw back a few pints. There was the controversial waiter buzzer that affixes to your table and allows you to summon your server at the touch of button; then there was Risk–Fashion Edition, the high-stakes board game of cashmere and condominiums. But, as with most inventions in a bar, they ended up on the floor with the peanut shells. That is, until *Cooking with Booze*.

We took our pub dream home to distill. The process became a game of experimentation—the recipes, ideas and flavor combinations poured out. There were disasters along the way but we forged ahead, driven by our successes and desire to create a guide that would marry our two vices: a book for those who love to eat and drink, for those who believe that wine, spirits and beer can be used as more than mere accompaniments to a meal.

Think of your liquor cabinet as an extension of your spice rack. Each bottle contains unique flavors and aromas that can't be replicated by herbs, extracts or other ingredients. These flavors add depth to dishes and work in virtually any type of cooking. *Cooking with Booze* is also about enjoying the process of preparing a meal. Every recipe includes a drink recommendation. We implore you to try these—each one has been carefully selected and *repeatedly* tested to ensure it complements the preparation of the dish.

We've also included a useful get-together section to help you host theme parties at home, ranging from a traditional Burns Supper with scotch sampling to a romantic Midsummer's Night Picnic. On pages 174–81 you'll find an invaluable index of alcohol that includes flavor notes, alcohol content and recommended substitutions. Our gift to you: the wisdom and tools to stagger forth, chin thrust forward, bottle held high, into the world of cuisine. You're very welcome.

Enough reading already! Get into your kitchen, crack open the refrigerator, raid the liquor cabinet and get cooking. You've got a lot of eating and drinking to do.

Cheers,

Ryan & Dave

Stand by Your Pan

ENJOYING A GLASS of wine or cocktail while preparing a meal is second nature, but before you cork that bottle, double check your ingredients and avoid a last-minute run to the store.

Always keep your guests entertained, but make sure you know how they're traveling and how much they're consuming. Plan ahead and have non-alcoholic alternatives available. And remember moderation is always the best policy.

NON-ALCOHOLIC ALTERNATIVES

There are various new cordials available in most grocery stores, these include elderflower, limeflower and ginger and lemongrass. Mixed with a splash of your favorite juice and topped up with soda these make a sophisticated adult cocktail with none of the hangover potential. Ensure you always have an alternative readily available.

ENTERTAIN RESPONSIBLY AND COOK SAFE

"A forgotten pan on the stove could mean disaster for you and your family. If someone in your household cooks or smokes while intoxicated, you must be aware of the risk. Keep a watchful eye on drinkers and make sure you have a working smoke alarm on every level of your home."

—Fire Marshall's Public Fire Safety Council
www.firesafetycouncil.com

STAND BY YOUR PAN.

Cooking is the #1 cause of home fires. Don't leave your cooking unattended. Keep an eye on your fries!

Alcohol Burn-off Chart

It's a common misconception that alcohol burns off completely in the cooking process but even after flambéing, 75% of the original alcohol content remains in the dish. Keep this in mind when you're preparing these recipes but also remember that when you break a dish down into six servings the amount of alcohol retained is actually small. Heating alcohol helps take away the harsh taste and allows the complex, rich flavors to enhance whatever you're preparing—thus Cooking with Booze. The chart below should help make things clear.

Preparation	Amount Retained
Added to boiling liquid and removed from heat	85%
Alcohol flamed	75%
No heat, stored overnight	70%
Baked 15 minutes	45%
Baked 25 minutes	40%
Baked 30 minutes	35%
Baked 1 hour	25%
Baked 1.5 hours	20%
Baked 2 hours	10%
Baked 2.5 hours	5%

Source: U.S. Department of Agriculture

BRUNCH

Brie and Pear Pastries *Hot Brown Cow* 13

Apple Cinnamon Muffins *Ciderhouse Tea* 14

Cranberry-Cointreau Scones *Almost Healthy Smoothies* 15

Buttermilk Pancakes with Boozy Bananas
Royal Mimosa 16

Grand Marnier French Toast
The Royals Hot Chocolate 18

Late Harvest Fruit Salad *Sunrise Spritzer* 19

Blueberry Waffles with Amaretto Syrup *Kenyan Sunrise* 21

Sparkling Wine with Mixed Berries *Sparkling Wine* 22

Yogurt and Granola with Strawberry Coulis
Coffee for a Crowd 25

Frittata with Sticky Bacon *Bloody Marys* 26

Coddled Eggs with Jägermeister and Brie *Fizzy Navel* 28

Chardonnay Poached Eggs with Emmenthal
Grapefruit Fizz 30

Brie and Pear Pastries

12 oz (350 g) brie at room temperature, rind removed

2 eggs plus 1 yolk

2 Tbsp (25 mL) Xanté Poire au Cognac or brandy

⅓ cup (75 mL) butter

¼ cup (50 mL) packed brown sugar

3 ripe but firm pears, peeled and sliced lengthwise

2 sheets (1 lb/500 g package) frozen puff pastry, thawed

1 Tbsp (15 mL) granulated sugar

MAKES 4 SERVINGS

Pastries for breakfast are a decadent treat, especially if you're trying to impress that special someone who stayed the night. Squeeze some fresh orange juice and deliver these just out of the oven for a warm breakfast in bed. If all goes according to plan you'll be spending the day under the covers. An added bonus is the leftovers.

COMBINE BRIE, 1 egg plus yolk and Xanté Poire au Cognac in food processor or medium bowl with hand-held mixer and blend until smooth. Refrigerate until ready to use.

Meanwhile, melt butter in skillet over medium-high heat, add sugar and cook for 1 minute. Add pears and cook for 1 to 2 minutes or until pears soften slightly. Remove from heat, transfer to clean bowl and refrigerate until cool.

Preheat oven to 450°F (230°C).

Roll 1 sheet of puff pastry into a 12- × 6-inch (30- × 15-cm) rectangle on a clean, lightly floured surface and cut into 2 equal squares. Repeat with second sheet. Set aside. Whisk remaining egg with 1 Tbsp (15 mL) of water until smooth. Spread equal amounts of brie mixture onto one-half of pastry squares, leaving ½-inch (1-cm) edge all around. Top with equal amounts of pear mixture. Brush inside edge of pastry with egg wash and fold pastry over to form a triangle. Make 3 slits in top of pastry with a paring knife, lightly brush with more egg wash and sprinkle with sugar.

Bake for 5 minutes then turn oven down to 375°F (190°C) and continue baking for 10 to 15 minutes or until pastry is golden brown and cooked through. Serve warm.

Hot Brown Cow

1 oz Kahlúa

5 oz steamed milk

COMBINE KAHLÚA and milk in a specialty coffee glass and sprinkle with cocoa, if desired.

Apple Cinnamon Muffins

½ cup (125 mL) raisins

1 red apple, peeled,
cored and chopped

⅓ cup (75 mL) Goldschläger

1¾ cups + 1 Tbsp (440 mL)
all-purpose flour

¾ cup (175 mL)
packed brown sugar

½ tsp (2 mL) salt

2 tsp (10 mL) baking powder

½ tsp (2 mL) ground allspice

⅓ cup (75 mL) vegetable oil

1 egg

⅓ cup (75 mL) milk

½ cup (125 mL)
granulated sugar

1½ tsp (7 mL)
ground cinnamon

½ cup (125 mL)
chilled, unsalted butter, cubed

MAKES 6 LARGE MUFFINS

Nothing says "home sweet home" like bickering siblings and apple cinnamon muffins. If these don't bring some peace to the family, just pass round the bottle.

SOAK RAISINS and apple in Goldschläger at room temperature overnight.

Preheat oven to 350°F (180°C).

Line muffin tin with 6 paper cups and lightly grease with cooking spray. Combine 1½ cups (375 mL) flour, brown sugar, salt, baking powder and allspice. Mix in oil, egg and milk. Fold in raisins and apples. Spoon batter into prepared muffin cups.

Stir together sugar, remaining flour and cinnamon in a small bowl. Add butter and combine with pastry cutter until a crumb consistency is reached. Sprinkle over unbaked muffins and bake for 25 to 30 minutes or until a toothpick inserted into center of muffin comes out clean.

Ciderhouse Tea

½ oz Goldschläger

2 oz apple cider

Hot tea

COMBINE GOLDSCHLÄGER and cider in a specialty coffee glass and top with hot tea. Garnish with a cinnamon stick, if desired.

Cranberry-Cointreau Scones

⅓ cup (75 mL) dried cranberries

2 Tbsp (25 mL) Cointreau

2 cups (500 mL) all-purpose flour

⅓ cup (75 mL) granulated sugar

2 tsp (10 mL) baking powder

Pinch salt

⅓ cup (75 mL) chilled, unsalted butter, cubed

½ cup + 1 Tbsp (140 mL) heavy cream (38%)

2 eggs

1 tsp (5 mL) vanilla

1 Tbsp (15 mL) grated orange zest

MAKES 8 SCONES

Scones—much like the British—are a little finicky and like structure. Luckily, the rules are simple: keep things cold, don't overmix and touch the dough as little as possible. This will prevent your scones from becoming gummy and dense, like Ryan in his old age.

SOAK CRANBERRIES in Cointreau at room temperature overnight.

Preheat oven to 375°F (190°C). Line a cookie sheet with parchment paper.

Whisk together flour, sugar, baking powder and salt in a large bowl. Add butter and blend into the flour mixture with a pastry cutter until the mixture has the consistency of coarse crumbs. In a small bowl combine ½ cup (125 mL) heavy cream, 1 egg and vanilla. Mix wet ingredients into dry mixture and add cranberries and orange zest. Stir until just combined, making sure not to overmix.

Knead dough gently on lightly floured surface until it just comes together. Roll out into a 7-inch (18-cm) circle and cut into 8 equal triangles. Place on prepared cookie sheet.

Whisk together remaining egg and 1 Tbsp (15 mL) cream. Brush mixture over scones and bake for 15 minutes or until lightly browned. Transfer to rack to cool. Serve with butter and jam, if desired.

Almost Healthy Smoothies

4 oz (125 mL) coconut rum

1 cup (250 mL) orange juice

1 cup (250 mL) pineapple juice

1 banana

1 cup (250 mL) plain yogurt

FILL BLENDER WITH ICE. Add rum, orange juice, pineapple juice, banana and yogurt and blend until smooth. Pour into chilled old-fashioned glasses and garnish with a spear of fresh pineapple, if desired. MAKES 4 SERVINGS.

Buttermilk Pancakes *with* Boozy Bananas

1¼ cups (300 mL)
all-purpose flour

1 Tbsp (15 mL) baking powder

1 Tbsp (15 mL) granulated sugar

½ tsp (2 mL) salt

⅓ cup + 1 Tbsp (90 mL) butter

1¾ cups (425 mL) buttermilk

1 egg

4 bananas

⅓ cup (75 mL)
packed brown sugar

¼ cup (50 mL) amber
or dark rum

½ tsp (2 mL) cinnamon

MAKES 4 SERVINGS

RUM RUNNING

Just as single malt scotches have gained popularity in the international market so too have ultra-premium and boutique rums. Craft-produced by traditional methods and aged for up to 12 years or longer, ultra-premium rums contain a flavor and intensity not found in their mass-market counterparts. Cruzan rum, from St. Croix in the U.S. Virgin Islands, features a single-barrel estate rum produced from a blend of aged rums which is then aged a second time in a single-oak cask. We suggest storing this rum in the bedroom, well away from the wandering hands of cola drinkers.

Since you can't pour rum on your breakfast cereal we recommend whipping up these pancakes to help take the edge off Sunday morning. Be warned—with this kind of start to your day Monday morning comes faster than you expect, so brew a strong pot of coffee!

PREHEAT OVEN TO 150°F (65°C).

Combine flour, baking powder, sugar and salt in large bowl. Melt 2 Tbsp (25 mL) butter. In a separate bowl whisk together buttermilk, egg and melted butter until smooth. Pour wet ingredients over flour mixture and whisk until smooth. Grease a large, non-stick skillet with just enough vegetable oil to coat the pan and place over medium heat until hot. Spoon batter onto skillet to form pancakes and cook until edges bubble and begin to dry. Flip and cook for an additional 2 minutes or until golden. Remove to baking dish and place in warm oven, and continue making pancakes until batter is used.

Meanwhile, slice bananas into ½-inch (1-cm) pieces and set aside. Melt remaining butter in medium non-stick skillet over medium heat. Add brown sugar and cook for 2 to 3 minutes or until sugar dissolves. Add rum and continue cooking for 2 minutes until a smooth syrup develops. Add bananas and cinnamon and cook for 1 to 2 minutes until bananas have softened slightly.

Arrange pancakes on plates and spoon over bananas and syrup. Serve immediately.

Royal Mimosa

Splash Chambord

2 oz orange juice

4 oz sparkling wine or champagne

POUR CHAMBORD and orange juice into champagne flute and top with sparkling wine.

Grand Marnier French Toast

6 eggs

½ cup (125 mL) light cream (18%)

2 Tbsp (25 mL) Grand Marnier

2 tsp (10 mL) orange zest

8 slices day-old baguette

MAKES 4 SERVINGS

STICKY FINGERS

The different grades of maple syrup are categorized by lightness of color and strength of flavor. This is largely dependent on when the maple syrup was harvested, weather and growing conditions for the trees during that year. Typically, lighter syrups are harvested earlier in the season. There's no right or wrong when choosing—it all depends on your taste.

Grade A Light Amber or Canada # 1 Light: Light in color with a delicate maple flavor. Traditional grade for serving on pancakes and widely used for making maple candies.

Grade A Medium Amber or Canada # 1 Medium: Darker and stronger maple flavor. Can be used for pancakes, waffles and baking.

Grade A Dark Amber or Canada #2 Amber: Very dark with a strong maple flavor. This grade is mostly used for cooking and baking.

Grade B or Canada #3 Dark: Sometimes called cooking syrup, it's very dark in color and has an extremely strong maple flavor and hints of caramel. Predominantly used in baked goods. Dark maple syrup usually accounts for only about 2% of maple syrup production.

French toast is one of the easiest breakfasts to pull together—even with one eye stuck closed and a jackhammer pounding inside your poor head. Serve this favorite with lots of maple syrup and charred breakfast sausages. It's best to use slightly dried-out bread and a very quiet skillet.

WHISK EGGS, cream, liqueur and zest together in a shallow baking dish. Grease a large skillet with butter and place over medium-high heat. Dip bread into egg mixture and cook for 3 to 4 minutes per side or until golden and cooked through.

The Royals Hot Chocolate

1½ cups (375 mL) steamed milk

1 oz chocolate syrup

½ oz Bailey's Irish Cream

½ oz white crème de menthe

COMBINE MILK, syrup and liqueurs in a specialty coffee glass and top with whipped cream and cinnamon, if desired.

Late Harvest Fruit Salad

**3 medium peaches,
peeled and sliced**

**2 Bartlett pears,
peeled and sliced**

**1 Granny Smith apple,
peeled and sliced**

1 Tbsp (15 mL) fresh lemon juice

1 cup (250 mL) fresh raspberries

**2 Tbsp (25 mL)
late harvest Riesling**

When the nights start to turn cool, summer produces some of its best tasting fruit. The flavors of peach, nectarine, apricot and melon pair wonderfully with late harvest Riesling so, before you cocoon for the winter, treat yourself and your guests to a final ray of sunshine.

COMBINE PEACH, pear and apple slices in medium bowl and toss with lemon juice. Add raspberries and wine and fold gently. Serve immediately or refrigerate for up to an hour. Serve with Greek yogurt or *fromage frais*, if desired.

MAKES 6 SERVINGS

Sunrise Spritzer

4 oz Gewürztraminer or Riesling (not late harvest)

1 oz cranberry juice

1 oz orange juice

Soda

FILL WINEGLASS WITH ICE, add wine and juices and top with soda. Garnish with fresh cranberries and an orange wheel, if desired.

MORE THAN ONE WAY TO SKIN A PEACH

Blanching is a quick and easy way to remove the skin from peaches or tomatoes and it saves your vegetable peeler for other things—like vegetables. Make an "X" in the bottom of the peach with a knife. Meanwhile, bring a stockpot of water to a boil and prepare an equally large bowl of ice water. Working with 2 peaches at a time, dunk the peaches into the boiling water for about 30 seconds then remove with a slotted spoon and immerse in bowl of cold water. Once cool use a paring knife to remove the skin.

Blueberry Waffles *with* Amaretto Syrup

4 eggs, separated

1 Tbsp (15 mL) granulated sugar

¼ cup (50 mL) butter, melted and cooled

1¼ cup (300 mL) milk

1 tsp (5 mL) vanilla

2 cups (500 mL) all-purpose flour

2 tsp (10 mL) baking powder

½ tsp (2 mL) salt

½ cup (125 mL) wild blueberries

1 cup (250 mL) pure
maple syrup (see page 18)

1 Tbsp (15 mL) amaretto

Easily identifiable by their piercings and tattoos, wild blueberries work best for waffles because they're smaller and have way more flavor than their domesticated cousins. If you can't find wild you can use tame, but it's best to use only fresh berries as the frozen ones can turn your breakfast purple.

PREHEAT WAFFLE IRON to high and brush with a little vegetable oil.

Whisk egg yolks with sugar in a large bowl until light and airy. Stir in melted butter, milk and vanilla. Add flour, baking powder and salt and beat well.

Whisk egg whites until stiff peaks form and gently fold into batter. Fold in blueberries. Spoon half the batter into waffle iron, close lid and cook for 5 to 7 minutes or until crisp. Repeat with remaining batter.

Meanwhile, combine maple syrup and amaretto. Serve over waffles.

MAKES 4 SERVINGS

Kenyan Sunrise

1 oz Amarula liqueur

5 oz brewed coffee

COMBINE AMARULA and coffee in a specialty coffee glass and garnish with a fresh strawberry, if desired.

Sparkling Wine *with* Mixed Berries

3 cups (750 mL) fresh
mixed berries
(raspberries, blueberries,
strawberries, blackberries,
red currants, etc.)

Sparkling wine

MAKES 6 SERVINGS

This dish elicits more oohs and ahhs than fireworks in July and is perfect for a celebratory brunch or even a light summer dessert. Champagne flutes make the best presentation but martini glasses or wineglasses will also work. Garnish with a sprig of mint or an orange twist and you'll get full Martha points.

QUARTER STRAWBERRIES (if using) and toss with other berries in a bowl. Fill glasses three-quarters full with berries and top with sparkling wine. Serve with tall parfait spoons or cocktail forks.

SPARKLING WINE 101

Champagne is from the Champagne region of France. Sparkling wine from anywhere else in the world can't use the name. Instead, it's called prosecco in Italy, cava in Spain, sekt in Germany and in the New World we call it what it is: sparkling wine. Sparkling wine is made when a little bit of sugar and yeast are left in the wine or added to the bottle before corking. The yeast ferments with the sugar and creates CO_2 bubbles that turn a normal bottle of wine into something of a weapon. Good times!

Yogurt and Granola *with* Strawberry Coulis

Break out the Birkenstocks and patchouli, we're off to the health food store! This recipe is for our nature-conscious readers and it contains barely enough booze to knot your dreadlocks. It's simple, portable and perfect for the start of an active day. Peace.

COMBINE YOGURT, honey and vanilla in a medium bowl and set aside. Combine strawberries, liqueur, sugar and lemon juice in blender and blend until smooth. Pour this coulis through a sieve to remove any seeds from strawberries.

Layer coulis, yogurt and granola in attractive glassware and serve with long spoons.

3 cups (750 mL) plain yogurt

½ cup (125 mL) honey

1 tsp (5 mL) vanilla

2 cups (500 mL) strawberries

1 Tbsp (15 mL) Chambord

2 tsp (10 mL) granulated sugar

1 tsp (5 mL) fresh lemon juice

3 cups (750 mL) granola

MAKES 6 SERVINGS

Coffee for a Crowd

⅓ cup (75 mL) freshly ground coffee

2 Tbsp (25 mL) unsweetened cocoa

1 cinnamon stick

4 cloves

Pinch nutmeg

1-inch (2.5-cm) piece lemon zest

1-inch (2.5-cm) piece orange zest

2 Tbsp (25 mL) packed brown sugar

4 oz white or dark rum

1 tsp (5 mL) vanilla

ADD COFFEE, cocoa, cinnamon stick, cloves, nutmeg, zest and sugar to coffee filter and brew 8 cups (2 L) coffee. Once brewed, add rum and vanilla to pot. MAKES 6 SERVINGS.

THIN RED LINE

For a perfect line between the strawberries and the yogurt pour the coulis in the glass and freeze for 20 minutes, or until firm. Spoon in yogurt and top with granola. Let stand at room temperature for 15 minutes before serving.

Frittata *with* Sticky Bacon

BASIC FRITTATA

1 Tbsp (15 mL) butter

8 eggs

¼ cup (50 mL) milk

½ tsp (2 mL) salt

FILLING OPTIONS

The Weekender

½ cup (125 mL) halved
grape tomatoes

½ cup (125 mL) grated Gruyère

¼ cup (50 mL) chopped
fresh basil

Uncle Jamie's Favorite

½ cup (125 mL) minced
red onion

½ cup (125 mL) chopped
smoked salmon

¼ cup (50 mL) crumbled
goat cheese

¼ cup (50 mL) chopped
fresh dill

Provençale

½ cup (125 mL) sliced
cremini mushrooms

½ cup (125 mL) cubed brie

¼ cup (50 mL) minced
red pepper

CONTINUED NEXT PAGE

Bacon and eggs are to breakfast as olives are to martinis. Put on the coffee and fire up the toaster. Combine the bacon with your own egg specialty or use one of the combos below.

PREHEAT OVEN TO BROIL.

Choose a filling option for the frittata. Melt butter in a large non-stick, ovenproof skillet over medium heat and sauté your first filling ingredient until softened, about 2 to 3 minutes. Lightly whisk eggs, milk and salt together in a large bowl and add remaining filling ingredients.

Add egg mixture to skillet and cook until set at the edge and underside is golden, about 6 to 7 minutes. Remove from heat and place on top rack under broiler and cook until top has set and is lightly browned, about 2 to 3 minutes. Serve either hot or at room temperature with sticky bacon.

To make the sticky bacon, cook bacon in a large skillet over medium-high heat until fat is reduced and bacon is almost crisp. Drain renderings and reduce heat to medium. Add maple syrup and whisky and cook until liquid thickens, about 1 minute. Serve with frittata.

Bloody Marys

¼ cup (50 mL) coarse salt

1 Tbsp (15 mL) freshly ground black pepper

4 lemon wedges

1 cup (250 mL) vodka

6 cups (1.5 L) tomato juice

1½ Tbsp (20 mL) Worcestershire sauce

1 Tbsp (15 mL) Tabasco sauce

1 tsp (5 mL) celery salt

4 stalks celery

COMBINE SALT AND PEPPER in a shallow bowl. Rub four Collins glasses with a lemon wedge and reserve for garnish. Dip each glass into salt mixture to coat rim.

Combine vodka, tomato juice, Worcestershire, Tabasco and celery salt in a 60 oz (2 L) pitcher. Fill glasses with ice and top with drink mix. Garnish with lemon wedges and celery stalks. SERVES 4 GENEROUSLY.

STICKY BACON

1 lb (500 g) bacon

¼ cup (50 mL) pure maple syrup (see page 18)

2 Tbsp (25 mL) Canadian whisky

MAKES 4 SERVINGS

Coddled Eggs *with* Jägermeister and Brie

8 slices fresh baguette

¼ cup (50 mL) butter

1 cup (250 mL) cremini
mushrooms, sliced

¾ cup (175 mL) shallots, minced

¾ cup (175 mL) fresh thyme,
finely chopped

¾ cup (175 mL) fresh baby
spinach, finely sliced

1 recipe caramelized
onions (page 112)

1 cup (250 mL) heavy cream
(38%)

½ cup (125 mL) Jägermeister

8 large eggs

6 oz (175 g) brie,
cut into 8 wedges

1 tsp (5 mL) cayenne pepper

Salt

Freshly ground black pepper

MAKES 8 SERVINGS

Everyone deserves a little coddling from time to time. Coddled eggs are an upscale yet easy to prepare alternative to everyday bacon and eggs. Creamy and sophisticated, they're guaranteed to make a breakfast special. You can prepare these up to three hours in advance—freeing up your hands for important hosting duties like serving berries and champagne.

PREHEAT OVEN to 325°F (160°C).

Butter baguette slices on both sides and place in bottom of 8 ramekins. Melt 1 Tbsp (15 mL) butter over medium heat in a medium-sized skillet, add mushrooms and shallots and cook for 3 to 4 minutes until shallots become translucent. Add thyme and spinach and season to taste with salt and pepper. Cook for an additional minute. Remove from heat and set aside.

Combine caramelized onions with mushroom mixture in a medium bowl. Distribute evenly between ramekins. Form a well in the center of each ramekin and crack an egg into each. Add 2 Tbsp (25 mL) cream and 1 Tbsp (15 mL) Jägermeister. Top with wedges of brie, a pinch of cayenne and salt and pepper. Place on baking sheet in center of oven and bake for 20 to 25 minutes or until egg whites are set but yolks are still soft.

Fizzy Navel

½ oz peach schnapps

4 oz fresh orange juice

Champagne

COMBINE SCHNAPPS and orange juice in a flute and top with champagne.

Chardonnay Poached Eggs *with* Emmenthal

1½ cups (375 mL) Chardonnay

8 eggs

8 slices fresh baguette

8 slices Emmenthal cheese

8 slices tomato

MAKES 4 SERVINGS

With less clean-up than its cousin, "Eggs Benny," this healthy breakfast is a fast fix for any fallout from the night before. Use fresh eggs because they stay together much better when poached. Feel free to add any vegetables you have on hand like sautéed onions, mushrooms or baby spinach.

FILL A DEEP SKILLET with wine, add enough water to bring level to 2 inches (5 cm) and bring to a gentle simmer. Crack eggs into a ladle or coffee mug and gently lower into hot water. Cook for 3 to 5 minutes or until whites are firm. Meanwhile, toast and butter baguette slices. Layer with cheese and tomato, crown with egg and garnish using your favorite herb, if desired.

Grapefruit Fizz

2 oz pink grapefruit juice

4 oz champagne

COMBINE GRAPEFRUIT JUICE and champagne in flute and garnish with a maraschino cherry, if desired.

APPETIZERS

Cabernet Tapenade

2 cups (500 mL) kalamata
olives, pitted

2 cloves garlic

2 anchovy fillets or
1 Tbsp (15 mL) anchovy paste

2 tsp (10 mL) capers

1 tsp (5 mL) freshly ground
black pepper

1 tsp (5 mL) dried tarragon

2 Tbsp (25 mL) extra
virgin olive oil

¼ cup (50 mL) Cabernet
Sauvignon

MAKES 2 1/2 CUPS (625 ML)

This versatile tapenade is perfect as a dip or a spread on anything you need to add a touch of class to (try hotdogs). The Cabernet mellows the saltiness of the olives, although any wine with hints of blackberry or plum will also add depth. Look for dry-cured olives. They look a little wrinkled, but don't let that put you off because they have the best flavor. This recipe is the backbone of the muffuletta sandwich (see page 151).

COMBINE OLIVES, garlic, anchovy, capers, pepper, tarragon, olive oil and wine and blend in food processor or blender until smooth. Serve with pita bread or toast points.

Summer Berry Sangria

1 bottle (750 mL) Cabernet (or remainder from tapenade recipe)

2 cups (500 mL) cranberry-raspberry juice

¼ cup (50 mL) granulated sugar

1 cup (250 mL) fresh cherries, sliced and pitted

1 cup (250 mL) fresh blackberries, sliced

1 orange, sliced

Soda

COMBINE WINE, juice, sugar, cherries, blackberries and orange slices in a large pitcher and stir until sugar dissolves. Refrigerate for at least 3 hours or overnight. Fill red wine glasses with ice, fill three-quarters full with sangria and top with soda. Garnish with an orange wheel, if desired. MAKES 4 SERVINGS.

CAPER CAPERS

Everyone seems to have an opinion on what a caper is (marine plant, member of the olive family or frog testicle) but few really know for sure. Capers are actually the bud of the caper plant (*Capparis spinosa*), an attractive wild shrub found across the Mediterranean. The buds are cleaned and pickled in brine. They add an intense salty bite to a dish and the smaller buds are generally more desirable.

Hummus *with* Pepper Vodka

Homemade hummus is easy to make and tastes much better than store-bought. Making it at home also means you can throw in as much garlic as you can handle, or you can add tasty extras like roasted red pepper and eggplant. It's equally great as a dip or sandwich spread and will last in the freezer for up to three months—long enough to complete a quality rehab program.

PURÉE GARLIC, olive oil and lemon juice with a hand-blender or food processor. Slowly add chickpeas, pepper vodka, tahini, salt, cumin, cayenne and white pepper and blend until smooth. Add 1 Tbsp (15 mL) of water at a time, if required, until desired consistency is reached.

Moscow Mule

1 oz vodka

½ oz fresh lime juice

Ginger beer

FILL A COLLINS GLASS WITH ICE. Add vodka, lime juice and top with ginger beer. Garnish with a slice of lime, if desired.

1 clove garlic

⅓ cup (75 mL) extra virgin olive oil

2 Tbsp (25 mL) fresh lemon juice

1 19-oz (540-mL) can chickpeas, rinsed and drained

2 Tbsp (25 mL) pepper vodka

1½ Tbsp (20 mL) tahini (sesame seed paste)

¼ tsp (1 mL) salt

Pinch ground cumin

Pinch cayenne

Pinch white pepper

MAKES 2 CUPS (500 ML)

OPEN SESAME

There are two varieties of sesame seed pastes: the Asian variety, called sesame butter, and the Middle Eastern variety, called tahini. The Asian variety is typically made with raw sesame seeds and the Middle Eastern with roasted sesame seeds. Both are readily available at major grocery stores and health food stores.

Lox, Stock and Capers

8 oz (250 g) cream cheese, softened

2 tsp (10 mL) crushed green peppercorns

1 Tbsp (15 mL) grated lemon zest

½ lb (250 g) thin-sliced Atlantic smoked salmon

¼ cup (50 mL) single malt scotch (Islay or Highland)

2 oz (60 g) red roe

1 Tbsp (15 mL) capers or 16 chive leaves

8 large, dark rye crackers (such as Ryvita Crispbread)

MAKES 8 APPETIZERS

Salty, smoky and sweet, this app is exactly what a crowd needs on a cold January evening. We assure you that these little gems will create such a lasting impression that you'll be doubling and tripling this recipe in coming years. Burns would be proud.

COMBINE CREAM CHEESE, peppercorns and zest in a medium bowl.

Place smoked salmon in a single layer in a shallow bowl or large plate and drizzle with scotch.

Spread 1 Tbsp (15 mL) of cream cheese mixture on each cracker. Roll pieces of smoked salmon into cones and place one on top of each cracker. Fill each cone with ½ tsp (2 mL) roe and garnish each cracker with a few capers or chives, if desired.

Old-Fashioned

1 sugar cube

2 dashes Angostura bitters

1¾ oz scotch

Orange zest

SOAK THE SUGAR CUBE with bitters in an old-fashioned glass and muddle with a bar spoon. Add a dash of scotch and a couple ice cubes and continue muddling the mixture, adding more scotch and ice until the full measure has been added to the glass. Run orange zest around the rim of the glass then drop it into the drink and serve.

Strawberries, Sambuca and Black Pepper

4 cups (1 L) strawberries

¼ cup (50 mL) sambuca

Freshly ground black pepper

MAKES 4–6 SERVINGS

Who would have guessed that strawberries, licorice and pepper would go together so well? And who would have guessed that three strawberries on a plate could look this pretentious? Feel free to be more generous and pile these high on a serving plate at your next cocktail party—a definite crowd-pleaser!

RINSE STRAWBERRIES under cold water and pat dry with paper towel. Pile onto serving plate or shallow bowl and pour over sambuca. Sprinkle with pepper to taste and serve.

Kir Royale

Dash cassis

6 oz champagne

ADD CASSIS TO CHAMPAGNE FLUTES and top with champagne.

Avocado, Prosciutto and Pepper

2 avocados, peeled and quartered

8 slices prosciutto

2 Tbsp (25 mL) fresh lemon juice

2 Tbsp (25 mL) extra
virgin olive oil

2 Tbsp (25 mL) pepper vodka

1 tsp (5 mL) lemon zest

Freshly ground black pepper

MAKES 4 SERVINGS

Fresh and light, this appetizer can be served home-style on a platter, or used to top a salad. It needs to be prepared just before serving because the avocado will brown if left too long. And make sure you save the pit—it makes a fantastic ping-pong ball.

WRAP AVOCADO QUARTERS in prosciutto. Combine lemon juice, olive oil and vodka and liberally brush wrapped avocado quarters. Sprinkle with lemon zest and season generously with pepper. Arrange 2 avocado quarters on each plate and serve immediately.

Lynchburg Lemonade

2 lemon wedges

2 tsp (10 mL) granulated sugar

1¾ oz Jack Daniel's

6 oz lemon-lime soda

SQUEEZE JUICE from lemon wedges into a Collins glass with sugar. Muddle lemon and sugar together with the end of a wooden spoon, until sugar dissolves. Fill with ice, add Jack Daniel's and top with soda. Garnish with lemon wheel, if desired.

Killa Crab Cakes

Who needs lobster when you can have crab? And, unlike "beefcakes" and "babycakes," crab cakes actually feature the real thing. Serve these yummy nibblies as appetizers, a tapas dish or a decadent accompaniment to a refreshing leafy green salad.

COMBINE CRABMEAT, egg, green onions, breadcrumbs, mustard, mayonnaise, lemon juice, hot pepper sauce, Worcestershire sauce and salt in a medium bowl and form into 8 crab cakes. Dredge through a shallow dish of breadcrumbs and refrigerate for at least 30 minutes.

Heat ½ inch (1 cm) of vegetable oil in a large deep skillet over medium-high heat until very hot, but not smoking. Fry crab cakes for 2 to 3 minutes per side or until golden. Serve with lime and horseradish mayo.

To make the mayo, combine mayonnaise, lime juice, horseradish, sherry, mustard, zest, hot pepper sauce, salt and pepper in a medium bowl and drop a spoonful on each crab cake. Mayo will keep in the refrigerator for up to a week.

Lemon Wedge

1½ oz lemon rum

½ oz Limoncello Di Leva

6 oz cranberry juice

Soda

COMBINE RUM, Limoncello Di Leva and cranberry juice in an ice-filled Collins glass, rimmed with sugar. Top with soda and garnish with lemon wedge, if desired.

CRAB CAKES

1 lb (500 g) crabmeat

1 egg, lightly beaten

6 green onions, white and green part, minced

½ cup (125 mL) dried breadcrumbs, plus more for rolling

1 Tbsp (15 mL) Dijon mustard

1 Tbsp (15 mL) mayonnaise

1 tsp (5 mL) fresh lemon juice

Dash hot pepper sauce

Dash Worcestershire sauce

Pinch salt

MAKES 4 SERVINGS

LIME AND HORSERADISH MAYO

¾ cup (175 mL) mayonnaise

1 Tbsp (15 mL) fresh lime juice

1 Tbsp (15 mL) horseradish

1 Tbsp (15 mL) sweet sherry

1 tsp (5 mL) hot mustard

1 tsp (5 mL) grated lime zest

¾ tsp (4 mL) hot pepper sauce

Pinch salt

Pinch freshly ground black pepper

MAKES 1 CUP (250 ML)

Vodka Salmon Nests

5 sheets phyllo pastry

3 Tbsp (45 mL) melted butter

3 Tbsp (45 mL) extra virgin olive oil

2 Tbsp (25 mL) fresh lemon juice

2 Tbsp (25 mL) vodka

2 tsp (10 mL) Worcestershire sauce

½ tsp (2 mL) cayenne

½ lb (250 g) thin-sliced smoked salmon, coarsely chopped

3 Tbsp (45 mL) red onion, minced

1 Tbsp (15 mL) capers

1 cup (250 mL) fresh dill, chopped

1 radicchio, leaves separated

MAKES 4 SERVINGS

PHUN WITH PHYLLO

Phyllo is a versatile paper-thin pastry that can be used for both sweet and savory dishes. Following the 3 tips below will ensure great results every time. Leftover phyllo can be stored in the freezer for about a month.

1. Defrost frozen phyllo overnight in the refrigerator. Defrosting at room temperature may cause condensation to form between the sheets and may cause them to stick together.

2. Prevent the phyllo from drying out by placing a clean, damp towel over it while working on a single sheet.

3. When assembling phyllo, brush each sheet with olive oil or clarified butter. For extra flavor, brush with brown butter—butter that is almost burnt.

There's something to be said about a fish that swims a hundred kilometers upstream only to perish—we'll drink to that and you should too. Vodka and salmon are natural partners: their flavors combine to create something wonderful. This recipe is to blame for starting this whole book thing and it's still one of our favorites.

PREHEAT OVEN TO 350°F (180°C). Coat 4 medium-sized ramekins (6 oz/175 mL) or muffin tins with cooking spray or melted butter.

Brush each sheet of phyllo with melted butter and stack one on top of the other. Cut phyllo layers into 4 equal squares and place each stack into a ramekin. Bake for 15 minutes or until edges are golden and pastry is crisp throughout. Remove from oven and place ramekins on rack to cool.

In a small bowl, combine olive oil, lemon juice, vodka, Worcestershire sauce and cayenne. Set aside. In a medium bowl, combine salmon, onion and capers. Add olive oil mixture and dill and toss well to combine.

Remove phyllo cups from ramekins and line each with a radicchio leaf. Fill cups with salmon mixture and serve.

Absolut Mojito

½ lime, quartered

1 tsp (5 mL) granulated sugar

2 sprigs fresh mint

1½ oz Absolut vodka

Soda

SQUEEZE JUICE from lime quarters into an old-fashioned glass. Toss in lime quarters, sugar and mint and muddle with the end of a wooden spoon until sugar is dissolved. Add vodka and top with soda. Garnish with a sprig of mint and a lime wheel, if desired.

Pinot Gris Steamed Mussels

1 lb (500 g) mussels,
beards removed

2 Tbsp (25 mL) butter

2 shallots, finely chopped

1 cup (250 mL) Pinot Gris

2 Tbsp (25 mL) cilantro,
finely chopped

MAKES 4–6 SERVINGS

This dish is perfect for steaming up the windows on a cold winter night (if you need the help, that is). Pinot Gris, with its harvest fruit flavors of peach, pear and apple, is divine with mussels. This combo doesn't need to be burdened by a myriad of spices or complicated ingredients. Just keep it simple.

IN A COLANDER, shake and rinse mussels under cold water, discarding any that remain open. Melt butter in large stockpot over medium heat. Add shallots and cook for 2 to 3 minutes until softened. Add wine and mussels, cover and steam over high heat until mussels open, about 4 to 5 minutes. Add cilantro and toss, discarding any unopened mussels.

Serve in large bowl with warm crusty bread and butter.

Pinot Gris

SERVE THIS DISH with the Pinot Gris remaining in the bottle. When that's finished, move on to a Gewürztraminer and, if you're ready for a third, try a Riesling. Each wine features similar flavors but with increasing sweetness—exactly the way any good night should go.

SEXY MUSSELS

When choosing mussels, make sure they are closed tightly or close quickly when tapped. Discard any that remain open, are loose or have chipped shells, missing teeth or lazy eyes. Store them wrapped in a moist towel in the fridge for no more than a day. Don't wrap them in plastic because they need air to breathe. Immediately before cooking, scrub the mussels with a vegetable brush under cold water and de-beard them if necessary. De-bearding is really just fancy talk for removing the threads that attached the mussels to their former home. Using a paring knife, pinch these threads between your thumb and the blade and pull toward the hinged point of the shell.

Bloody Caesar Steamed Mussels

The Bloody Caesar is one of those drinks that's bloody perfect for any bloody occasion. This seafood creation is inspired by the classic Canadian drink and even we have to admit, it's bloody genius. Dispose of any mussels that don't open and beware the Ides of March.

IN A COLANDER, shake and rinse mussels under cold water, discarding any that remain open. Heat oil in large stockpot over medium heat. Add onion and garlic and cook for 2 to 3 minutes until softened. Add Clamato juice, vodka, tomatoes, celery leaves, lemon, horseradish, Worcestershire sauce, celery salt, Tabasco sauce and black pepper. Cover and steam over high heat until mussels open, about 4 to 5 minutes.

Transfer to bowl and serve with warm crusty bread or spoon over cooked linguini for a complete meal.

The Perfect Caesar

Celery salt

1½ oz vodka

2 dashes Worcestershire sauce

Dash Tabasco sauce

½ tsp (2 mL) horseradish

6 oz Clamato juice

Salt

Freshly ground black pepper

Celery stick

Lemon wedge

RIM A COLLINS GLASS with celery salt and fill with ice, vodka, Worcestershire sauce, Tabasco and horseradish. Top with Clamato. Garnish with salt, pepper, celery stick and lemon wedge.

1 lb (500 g) mussels, beards removed (see page 42)

2 Tbsp (25 mL) extra virgin olive oil

1 small onion, finely chopped

2 cloves garlic, minced

1 cup (250 mL) Clamato juice

¼ cup (50 mL) vodka

2 plum tomatoes, chopped

2 Tbsp (25 mL) chopped celery leaves

1 Tbsp (15 mL) fresh lemon juice

2 tsp (10 mL) horseradish

1 tsp (5 mL) Worcestershire sauce

½ tsp (2 mL) celery salt

Dash Tabasco sauce

Freshly ground black pepper

MAKES 4–6 SERVINGS

French Quarter Coconut Shrimp

The Big Easy remains synonymous with hedonism—eating, drinking and flashing strangers for Mardi Gras beads. This New Orleans-inspired combo meets two of those requirements but the third is up to you.

PREHEAT OVEN TO 400°F (200°C). Spray large rimmed baking sheet with cooking spray.

Season shrimp with salt, pepper and garlic powder. Put eggs, flour and coconut into 3 separate bowls. Dip shrimp into egg, then flour, then again in egg and finally into coconut. Arrange shrimp on baking sheet and bake for 12 to 15 minutes or until golden and crisp.

Arrange on serving platter with bourbon dipping sauce.

To make the sauce, reduce bourbon by one-third in a small saucepan over medium-high heat. Add corn syrup, molasses and pepper flakes. Bring to a boil, reduce heat and simmer for 5 minutes. Remove from heat and transfer to serving dish. Sauce will thicken slightly as it cools.

Hurricane

1 oz dark rum

1 oz white rum

2 oz orange juice

2 oz pineapple juice

½ oz grenadine

COMBINE RUM, orange juice, pineapple juice and grenadine in a cocktail shaker filled with ice and shake vigorously. Strain into an ice-filled Collins glass and garnish with an orange slice and a cherry, if desired.

SHRIMP

1 lb (500 g) extra-large shrimp (16–20 count), peeled and deveined, tail on

¼ tsp (1 mL) salt

Pinch freshly ground black pepper

Pinch garlic powder

3 eggs, beaten

1½ cups (375 mL) all-purpose flour

2½ cups (625 mL) shredded sweetened coconut

BOURBON SAUCE

½ cup (125 mL) bourbon

¼ cup (50 mL) light corn syrup

2 Tbsp (25 mL) fancy molasses

Pinch hot pepper flakes

MAKES 4–6 SERVINGS

CUCKOO FOR COCONUTS

If your bowl of coconut starts to clump, sprinkle with 1 Tbsp (15 mL) flour to loosen. Repeat if necessary.

Lime Tequila Peel-and-Eat Shrimp

1 lb (500 g) extra-large shrimp
(16–20 count), deveined, shell on

3 Tbsp (45 mL) tequila

2 cloves garlic minced

2 Tbsp (25 mL) fresh lime juice

2 tsp (10 mL) lime zest

¼ tsp (1 mL) hot pepper flakes

3 Tbsp (45 mL) butter

MAKES 4–6 SERVINGS

This hands-on summer app is simple and delicious—perfect for serving to friends who drop by with a bottle of Tijuana's finest and a bag of fresh limes. Prepare it on the side burner of your gas grill and flambé if you dare!

COMBINE SHRIMP, tequila, garlic, lime juice, lime zest and pepper flakes in a medium bowl. Cover and refrigerate for 15 to 30 minutes. Melt butter in a large skillet over medium-high heat. Add shrimp and cook until firm and bright pink, about 2 to 3 minutes. Transfer to serving dish and enjoy.

Caribbean Spritzer

4 oz Sauvignon Blanc

½ oz limeflower cordial (or squeeze of fresh lime juice)

Soda

FILL WHITE WINEGLASS WITH ICE. Add wine and lime and top with soda.

SHRINKAGE

Shrimp are divided into three basic categories: cold water, typically from the Atlantic; warm water or tropical; and freshwater, usually farm-raised in lakes and streams. The colder the water, the smaller the shrimp—but who can't relate to that?

Shrimp are sold in quantity per pound measurements that are referred to as count. An 11 to 15 count, for example, is the number of shrimp per pound. The counts are then categorized as follows.

COUNT
(SHRIMP PER POUND)

10 shrimp or less = Colossal
11 to 15 = Jumbo
16 to 20 = Extra-large
21 to 30 = Large
31 to 35 = Medium
36 to 45 = Small
46 plus = Miniature

Oyster Shooters

24 oysters

1 bottle (750 mL) Sauvignon Blanc

Shot glasses

Oysters (like old-world wines) are almost always named after the location they're harvested—Malpeques from Malpeque Bay, Prince Edward Island; Blue Points from Blue Point, Long Island, etc. The geographical differences in marine life, food sources, salt content and water temperature all affect their flavor.

Oysters are best during the "R" months, so don't plan your shooter party from May through August. That's when the little guys get it on and, as with any oversexed creature, their texture can become gritty and coarse.

TOOLS:

oyster shucker or any sturdy, blunt knife, tea towel and cutting board.

MAKES 24 OYSTERS

PLACE EACH OYSTER on cutting board and cover with towel. Hold oyster firmly and slip the knife blade between top and bottom shell at the hinge of the oyster. Twist knife slowly until shells separate, push the knife in further and run it along the top shell to release it. Remove top shell and use the knife to separate the oyster from the bottom shell. If this fails, we suggest high-speed rotary power tools and protective eyewear.

Place shucked oysters into shot glasses. Fill glasses with Sauvignon Blanc and shoot like a rock star.

Gibson

Dash dry vermouth

2½ oz gin

2 pearl onions

RINSE MARTINI GLASS with vermouth, then discard vermouth. Shake gin vigorously in a cocktail shaker filled with ice then strain into martini glass. Garnish with onions.

EAST MEETS WEST

You can easily identify whether your oyster is from the east or west coast. West coast oysters have scalloped shells and a more relaxed attitude while east coast oysters are flat shelled, abrupt and straight to the point.

SAFFRON ECONOMICS

Saffron, the world's most precious and expensive spice, is the dried stigmas of the saffron flower (*Crocus sativus*). Each flower contains only 3 stigmas and must be picked by hand. It takes over 75,000 flowers to produce 1 pound (500 g) of saffron and in 2004, Iran, the world's largest exporter of saffron, exported more than 147 tons of it.

Saffron is revered for its ability to turn sauces and rice dishes a beautifully bright yellow color while adding a subtle tea-like flavor. Its strong coloring power and intense flavor means that it can be used sparingly.

Pan-Seared Scallops *with* Swahili Sauce

This West African sauce is a rich combination of flavors— a result of much shameless borrowing from East Indian neighbors. We suggest exploiting the advice of our Thai friends and matching the creamy richness with an ice-cold lager, but a fruity, frozen concoction is also good. Serve over pasta for a complete meal.

FOR THE SAUCE, melt butter in a large skillet over medium-heat, add onion and cook until softened, approximately 3 to 4 minutes. Add garlic, cumin, salt, pepper, turmeric and saffron and cook for 1 minute longer. Add tomatoes, tomato paste and wine, bring to boil, then stir in coconut milk and cilantro. Reduce heat and simmer until slightly thickened, about 10 minutes.

Meanwhile, pat scallops dry with paper towel and season with salt, pepper and orange zest. Heat oil in large non-stick skillet over medium-high heat until it begins to smoke. Add scallops and cook until seared, about 1 to 2 minutes. Turn and sear second side, about 2 minutes.

Spoon sauce onto small plates, top with 3 scallops per person and serve immediately.

Singha

TRY THIS DISH with an Asian lager like Singha, from Thailand. Its lemon, cinnamon and floral notes complement the sauce perfectly.

SWAHILI SAUCE

2 Tbsp (25 mL) butter

1 small onion, minced

1 clove garlic, minced

½ tsp (2 mL) ground cumin

½ tsp (2 mL) salt

¼ tsp (1 mL) freshly ground black pepper

¼ tsp (1 mL) turmeric

Pinch saffron

1 28-oz (796-mL) can chopped tomatoes, drained

2 tsp (10 mL) tomato paste

¼ cup (50 mL) Chenin Blanc or Chardonnay

1 cup (250 mL) coconut milk

¼ cup (50 mL) cilantro, chopped

SCALLOPS

18 large sea scallops

½ tsp (2 mL) salt

Pinch freshly ground black pepper

1 tsp (5 mL) orange zest

1 Tbsp (15 mL) vegetable oil

MAKES 6 SERVINGS

Apricot and Vanilla Chicken Baskets

12 wonton wrappers

2 Tbsp (25 mL) extra virgin olive oil

1 boneless, skinless chicken breast, finely chopped

2 cloves garlic, minced

2 Tbsp (25 mL) soy sauce

2 Tbsp (25 mL) fresh lemon juice

1 tsp (5 mL) ground cumin

1 tsp (5 mL) grated fresh ginger

½ tsp (2 mL) freshly ground black pepper

½ cup (125 mL) apricot jam

1 Tbsp (15 mL) apricot brandy

1 tsp (5 mL) vanilla

1 hot red chili with seeds, finely sliced

1 Tbsp (15 mL) chopped cilantro

2 green onions, sliced

MAKES 12 SERVINGS

These hors d'oeuvres are perfect for any special occasion—New Year's Eve, college graduation, successful vasectomy—and are the perfect balance between sweet and savory. The addition of vanilla helps round out the flavors and adds an amazing aroma. See, things are looking up already.

PREHEAT OVEN TO 350°F (180°C). Coat 12 mini muffin cups with cooking spray and line each cup with a wonton sheet.

Lightly spray wonton sheets and bake for about 6 to 8 minutes or until golden. Remove from oven and allow to cool before removing from tins.

Heat oil over medium-high heat in a medium-sized skillet, add chicken, garlic, soy sauce, lemon juice, cumin, ginger and black pepper. Cook for about 7 minutes, or until chicken is cooked through. Add jam, brandy, vanilla, chili, cilantro and green onion and stir until sauce is smooth. Remove from heat and set aside to cool slightly.

Spoon chicken mixture into wonton cups and garnish with more chilies and cilantro sprigs, if desired. Serve immediately.

Mangopolitan

1½ oz mango vodka

½ oz Cointreau

¾ oz fresh lime juice

¾ oz cranberry juice

COMBINE VODKA, Cointreau, lime juice and cranberry juice in a cocktail shaker filled with ice and shake vigorously. Strain into a chilled martini glass and garnish with an orange twist, if desired.

Old Cheddar and Cider Fondue

2 cloves garlic, halved

1 lb (500 g) old cheddar, shredded

½ cup (125 mL) dry cider

1 Tbsp (15 mL) cornstarch

Pinch cayenne

1 baguette,
cut into bite-size pieces

MAKES 4–6 SERVINGS

There's no food more social than fondue, and sitting around a big pot of bubbling cheese is always a good idea. It's the perfect opportunity to touch forks with that certain someone across the table. You can substitute beer for the cider, but the crisp apple flavor of the cider mellows the sharp bite of the cheddar. The drier the cider, the better.

RUB FONDUE POT with one clove of garlic and discard garlic. Combine the other clove of garlic with cheese, cider, cornstarch and cayenne in a medium saucepan over medium-low heat, stirring constantly until melted. Transfer to fondue pot and serve with bread. Green apple slices are also great with this fondue.

Deep 6

As you sip on this drink the Southern Comfort slowly seeps into your beer, adding a sweet kick to an otherwise ordinary bevy.

1 oz Southern Comfort

1 12-oz (341-mL) bottle ale

POUR SOUTHERN COMFORT into a shot glass. Place an inverted pilsner glass over the shot by holding the shot against the inside base of the pilsner glass. Turn both glasses right-side up, trapping the shot on the bottom of the pilsner glass. Carefully pour beer over inverted shot glass. The liqueur will seep into the beer as you drink it.

Ryan and Dave's Party Balls

Okay, so meatballs get a bad rap, especially in today's chickpea and tofu world, but when it comes down to it, just about every carnivore loves a good meatball and these are the best we've ever tasted. Take off your slipper and prepare to beat back the vegetarians.

PREHEAT OVEN TO 350°F (180°C). Lightly grease cookie sheet or broiler pan.

To make the party balls combine beef, pork, onion, eggs, breadcrumbs, parsley and salt and pepper and mix until just combined. Shape into bite-size balls and place on cookie sheet or broiler pan. Bake for 10 to 15 minutes or until golden brown. Remove from oven and drain on paper towel.

Meanwhile, melt butter in large saucepan over medium heat. Add shallots, stirring until soft, about 3 minutes. Add cranberries, jelly and mustard and continue cooking until melted and well blended.

In a small bowl dissolve cornstarch in water and add to pot with orange juice, scotch and lemon juice. Cover and bring just to a boil. Add meatballs, reduce heat and simmer for at least an hour but the longer the better!

Cosmopolitan

If you're going to serve manly meatballs why not mess with your guests' heads and mix up some girlie martinis. Opposites attract.

> 2 oz vodka
>
> 1 oz cranberry juice
>
> Dash Cointreau
>
> Dash fresh lime juice

COMBINE VODKA, cranberry juice, Cointreau and lime juice in a cocktail shaker filled with ice and shake vigorously. Strain into a chilled martini glass and garnish with an orange twist, if desired.

MEATBALLS

1½ lb (750 g) ground beef

1½ lb (750 g) ground pork

1 medium onion, minced

2 eggs, lightly beaten

½ cup (125 mL) dried breadcrumbs

2 Tbsp (25 mL) chopped fresh parsley

2 tsp (10 mL) salt

½ tsp (2 mL) freshly ground black pepper

SWEET 'N' BOOZY SAUCE

2 Tbsp (25 mL) butter

4 shallots, minced

⅓ cup (75 mL) dried cranberries, chopped

¼ cup (50 mL) red currant jelly

1 Tbsp (15 mL) Dijon mustard

1 Tbsp (15 mL) cornstarch

¼ cup (50 mL) water

1½ cups (375 mL) fresh orange juice

½ cup (125 mL) scotch

¼ cup (50 mL) fresh lemon juice

MAKES ABOUT 80 BITES

Cajun Wings *with* Dijon Drambuie Dip

DIJON DRAMBUIE DIP

¾ cup (175 mL) mayonnaise

¼ cup (50 mL) Dijon mustard

¼ cup (50 mL) Drambuie

Pinch hot pepper flakes

WINGS

2 lb (1 kg) chicken wings

2 Tbsp (25 mL) extra virgin olive oil

1 Tbsp (15 mL) chili powder

1 Tbsp (15 mL) dried onion

1 Tbsp (15 mL) dried oregano

1 Tbsp (15 mL) dried thyme

1 tsp (5 mL) cayenne

1 tsp (5 mL) salt

1 tsp (5 mL) paprika

1 tsp (5 mL) garlic powder

1 tsp (5 mL) freshly ground black pepper

MAKES 4 SERVINGS

If you're like us and hate wings dripping in sauce, then this recipe is for you. But we recognize that some people like a little sauce with their chicken and so, as your humble servants, we've included a dip. It happens to be the same color as your refrigerator from the '70s but it tastes so damn good we're willing to let that slide.

TO MAKE THE DIP, combine mayonnaise, Dijon, Drambuie and hot pepper flakes in a small bowl and whisk until smooth. Cover and refrigerate until ready to use.

Preheat oven to broil and spray broiler pan with cooking spray.

Toss wings in olive oil to coat. Combine spices and toss with wings in a large bowl until evenly coated. Arrange fat-side down on pan and broil for 45 minutes or until crispy, turning wings halfway through cooking time. Transfer to platter and serve with dip.

Craft-Brewed Beer

AS GOOD CANADIAN BOYS, we know you can't eat wings without beer. Leave the big breweries behind for a night and explore some unique craft-brewed beers—coffee porter, raspberry wheat or Belgium white. The perfect beer is out there but you won't find it until you've experimented with a few along the way.

Beer Crostini *with* Figs and Gorgonzola

CROSTINI

1 12-oz (341-mL) bottle lager

1 baguette,
sliced into 24 pieces

¼ cup (50 mL) extra
virgin olive oil

FIGS AND GORGONZOLA

8 figs (fresh or dried)

2 Tbsp (15 mL) port

1 Tbsp (25 mL) extra
virgin olive oil

2 Tbsp (25 mL)
balsamic vinegar

½ tsp (2 mL) salt

½ tsp (2 mL) freshly
ground black pepper

¼ cup (50 mL)
crumbled gorgonzola

MAKES 24 PIECES

It makes sense that the yeasty flavor of beer goes so well with fresh bread. The only real trick is to make sure you don't soak the bread too long—all it needs is a quick dip and you're ready to go.

PREHEAT OVEN TO BROIL.

Pour lager into shallow baking dish and lightly dip bottom side of bread into beer (bread should be moist but not soaked through). Brush top with olive oil and toast under broiler until golden brown, turning once, about 8 to 10 minutes.

Slice figs into thirds and combine in shallow bowl with port, olive oil, vinegar and salt and pepper. (This can be done in advance and refrigerated overnight.)

Top cooked crostini with a slice of fig and some gorgonzola. Transfer to a lined baking sheet and broil on top rack of oven for 2 to 3 minutes or until cheese is melted.

OTHER SUGGESTED FIXIN'S: Cabernet Tapenade (page 32) with charred pineapple wedges and Oka or roast chicken with pesto and sundried tomatoes.

Havana Beach

1½ oz white rum

4 oz pineapple juice

Splash fresh lemon juice

COMBINE RUM, pineapple juice and lemon juice in an old-fashioned glass filled with ice. Garnish with lime wedge, if desired.

SOUPS AND SIDES

Roasted Red Pepper Gazpacho

3 large ripe tomatoes

1 Tbsp (15 mL) extra virgin olive oil

1 cup (250 mL) sliced green onions, white and green parts

1 cup (250 mL) zucchini, sliced

2 cloves garlic, minced

1 roasted red pepper, chopped (see sidebar below)

½ tsp (2 mL) hot pepper sauce

1½ cups (375 mL) chicken stock

¼ cup (50 mL) dry Riesling

¼ cup (50 mL) vodka

Salt

Freshly ground black pepper

MAKES 4 SERVINGS

We think gazpacho roughly translates to cold tomato soup, but we didn't look it up—that's your assignment for today. This soup is worth making even if you only plan to use it for the drink recipe below. Talk about a liquid lunch.

SLICE AN "×" into the bottom of each tomato. Blanch them in boiling water for 30 seconds and immediately transfer to a bowl filled with cold water. Remove skins and seeds and coarsely chop tomatoes to produce about 1 ¼ cups (300 mL). Drain and reserve liquid.

Heat oil in a large skillet over medium heat. Sauté green onions, zucchini and garlic, stirring constantly for 3 to 4 minutes or until softened. Stir in tomatoes, roasted pepper and hot pepper sauce and cook for 2 to 3 minutes. Add stock and bring to a simmer.

Remove from heat and stir in wine, vodka and any reserved tomato liquid. Purée with hand-held blender or in batches in a traditional blender. Cover and refrigerate overnight. Season to taste with salt and pepper.

Spiked Gazpacho

1 oz pepper vodka

4 oz Roasted Red Pepper Gazpacho

SHAKE VODKA and gazpacho together in a cocktail shaker filled with ice then pour into martini glass. Garnish with sprig of parsley, if desired.

PECK O' PEPPERS

To roast peppers, brush with a little olive oil and roast on a hot grill or in an oven preheated to 450°F (230°C) until skins are charred. Place in a bowl and cover with plastic wrap until cool. Remove skins, seeds and core. Peppers will keep in the refrigerator for up to a week.

Carrot, Ginger and Drambuie Soup

This soup is like a fireplace in a bowl. It's perfect when you need a little warming up on a chilly winter night, and if you make it like David does, with a heavy pinch of cayenne, it'll keep you warm right through the season (that is, if you don't have someone to do that for you).

MELT BUTTER IN LARGE SKILLET over medium-high heat. Add carrots, onions and ginger and sauté for 5 minutes or until onions are translucent. Reduce heat to medium and continue cooking until water has evaporated and carrots begin to caramelize (that is, begin to brown and stick to bottom of pan).

Deglaze pan with chicken stock and add bay leaves. Bring to a boil, reduce heat and let simmer 20 minutes.

Remove bay leaves, add orange juice, sugar, salt and cayenne and purée with hand-held blender or in batches in a traditional blender. Add light cream and simmer gently for 15 minutes. Add Drambuie and simmer for an additional 5 minutes.

Ladle into soup bowls and garnish with a dollop of sour cream and cilantro (if using).

Rob Roy

1 oz scotch

1 oz sweet vermouth

2 dashes Angostura Bitters

COMBINE SCOTCH, vermouth and bitters in a cocktail shaker filled with ice and shake vigorously. Strain into a chilled martini glass and garnish with an orange twist, if desired.

3 Tbsp (45 mL) butter

2 lb (1 kg) carrots, peeled and chopped

2 large onions, chopped

2 Tbsp (25 mL) minced fresh ginger

2 cups (500 mL) chicken stock

3 bay leaves

2 cups (500 mL) orange juice

2 Tbsp (25 mL) granulated sugar

1 Tbsp (15 mL) salt (or to taste)

¼ tsp (1 mL) cayenne

1½ cups (375 mL) light cream (18%)

⅓ cup (75 mL) Drambuie

⅓ cup (75 mL) sour cream (optional)

Cilantro sprigs (optional)

MAKES 6 SERVINGS

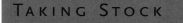

TAKING STOCK

Nothing can replace the taste of homemade stock, but thankfully store-bought options have come a long way. Prepared stocks have evolved from the days of bouillon cubes offering flavors like "brown." Today's hermetically sealed, shelf-stable, pre-packaged stocks are great alternatives. Also, visit your butcher shop to see if they offer a range of freshly made stocks.

THE SQUEEZE ON OLIVE OIL

Olive oil can generally be categorized as refined or unrefined. Unrefined olive oil is obtained from cold-pressing of olives prior to the use of other extraction agents such as pressure, heat or chemicals.

PREMIUM OR EXTRA VIRGIN OLIVE OIL: Is unrefined and obtained from the first pressing of the olives. It's ideal for drizzling over soups, salads, appetizers or breads, but it's not suited for frying.

VIRGIN OLIVE OIL: Is unrefined and has a slightly higher acidity level than extra virgin. It's more suited to sautéing, pan frying or broiling.

PURE OLIVE OIL: Is a blend of refined and virgin oils and is suitable for deep-frying.

LIGHT OLIVE OIL: Is refined through a filtering process that makes it lighter in color and fragrance and milder in flavor. Light olive oil is good for baking or frying, but it's not any lower in calories than the other types of olive oil.

Cauliflower and Herb Soup

Like the gawky, awkward kid in gym class, cauliflower is always picked last from the crudités platter. But before you turn the page, you should know that this soup brings out cauliflower's best quality—a delicate, earthy flavor. Semillon, also known for its terrestrial undertones, makes this soup smooth and sophisticated. Show some compassion and save cauliflower from its cheese-sauce drowning.

HEAT 3 TBSP (45 ML) OF OIL in a medium stockpot over medium-high heat. Add chicken thighs and sauté, stirring occasionally for 10 minutes or until chicken is browned. Remove chicken and set aside. Add onion and garlic and sauté until softened, about 3 to 4 minutes.

Deglaze pan by adding Semillon and 1 cup (250 mL) water. Add chicken stock and bay leaves and bring to a rolling boil. Add chicken thighs and reduce heat to medium-low. Simmer, partially covered, for 30 minutes. Remove chicken and save for another use.

Add cauliflower, salt, pepper, rosemary and thyme to soup and simmer for an additional 25 minutes. Remove bay leaves and discard. Remove soup from heat and purée with hand-held blender, or in batches in traditional blender. Return to heat, add cream and thin with water, if necessary. Simmer gently until ready to serve.

Heat remaining oil in a small skillet over medium heat. Tear prosciutto into small pieces and sauté until crisp. Fill bowls with soup and garnish with prosciutto.

¼ cup (50 mL) extra virgin olive oil

4 chicken thighs, skinned

1 sweet white onion, chopped

2 garlic cloves, minced

1 cup (250 mL) Semillon

2 cups (500 mL) chicken stock

2 bay leaves

1 large cauliflower head, chopped into florets

1 tsp (5 mL) salt

½ tsp (2 mL) freshly ground black pepper

½ tsp (2 mL) dried rosemary

1 tsp (5 mL) dried thyme

2 Tbsp (15 mL) heavy cream (38%)

4 slices prosciutto

MAKES 6 SERVINGS

Moving Sideways

2 oz vodka

½ oz dry vermouth

Dash Angostura Bitters

COMBINE VODKA, vermouth and bitters in cocktail shaker filled with ice, shake vigorously and strain into chilled martini glass. Garnish with an orange twist, if desired.

Lobster Bisque *with* Cognac Cream

LOBSTER BISQUE

1 bottle (750mL) Chardonnay

1 onion, finely chopped

1 stalk celery, finely chopped

2 bay leaves

2 live lobsters
(1½ lb/750 g) each

2 cups (500 mL)
light cream (18%)

3 Tbsp (45 mL) tomato paste

2 Tbsp (25 mL) sweet sherry

1 Tbsp (15 mL) finely
chopped chives

2 tsp (10 mL) chopped
fresh tarragon

Salt

Freshly ground black pepper

COGNAC CREAM (OPTIONAL)

1 cup (250 mL)
heavy cream (38%)

2 Tbsp (25 mL) cognac

Dash hot pepper sauce

Salt

MAKES 4–6 SERVINGS

Nothing screams decadence like lobster and cream. And while the garnish is optional, a little dollop of spiked cream elevates this dish to culinary heaven. Skip dessert if it makes you feel better.

COMBINE WINE, onion, celery and bay leaves in a large stockpot and bring to a simmer over medium heat. Cook for 5 minutes then increase heat to medium-high, add the lobsters, cover and cook for 10 minutes. Turn heat off and remove lobsters from stock and place in a bowl to cool.

With the stock sitting over medium heat, whisk 1 Tbsp (15 mL) cream into the tomato paste until smooth. Continue adding cream a little at a time until it is all incorporated into the tomato paste. Whisk cream mixture into the stock and remove from heat.

Crack lobsters, remove meat from claws and tail and chop. Set aside. Break up shells and add to soup. Return to heat and simmer uncovered for 20 to 30 minutes, or until soup has reduced to your preferred consistency, then remove shells and pour soup through a fine sieve. Return to pot, add sherry, herbs and lobster meat and simmer just until heated through. Season with salt and pepper to taste. Spoon into bowls and garnish with cognac cream (if using) and some chives, if desired.

To make the cognac cream, combine heavy cream, cognac and hot pepper sauce in medium bowl and beat with hand-held mixer until soft peaks form. Season to taste with salt and refrigerate until ready to use. MAKES ABOUT 2 CUPS (500 ML)

French Kiss

Dash of cognac

6 oz champagne

ADD COGNAC TO FLUTE and top with champagne.

Infamous German Potato Salad

6 medium new potatoes

6 slices bacon

½ medium fennel bulb, chopped

1 Tbsp (15 mL) Pernod

¼ cup (50 mL) white wine vinegar

2 tsp (10 mL) grain or Dijon mustard

2 Tbsp (25 mL) vegetable oil

6 green onions, finely sliced

2 Tbsp (25 mL) chopped fennel leaves

1 tsp (5 mL) salt

½ tsp (2 mL) freshly ground black pepper

MAKES 6 SERVINGS

Straight from the fatherland of sleek vehicles, extreme tidiness and the biggest celebration of beer in the universe, we give you German potato salad. With a little kick of Pernod from its French neighbors and a smack of fennel, this is anything but traditional German fare. Ein Prosit!

SCRUB POTATOES under cold water to remove excess dirt. Cook in boiling salted water until tender but still firm, about 20 minutes. Remove from heat and rinse under cold water to stop the cooking process. Drain and let cool completely. Slice potatoes into bite-size pieces.

Cook bacon in a medium-sized non-stick skillet over medium heat until crisp. Transfer to paper towel to drain, then crumble. Add fennel to pan with bacon renderings and cook until slightly tender, about 2 to 3 minutes. Reduce heat, add Pernod, vinegar, mustard and oil. Cook for 1 minute longer. Remove from heat and toss with potatoes. Add green onions, bacon and fennel leaves. Season with salt and pepper.

Orange Ice

2 oz vodka

1 oz Sour Puss Tangerine

Dash triple sec

6 oz lemon-lime soda

COMBINE VODKA, liqueurs and soda in a Collins glass filled with ice and garnish with an orange wheel, if desired.

Soul of the Vine Salad

When the summer heat becomes too intense, step into air-conditioned comfort with a cool and refreshing vine-ripened salad. Serve on chilled plates with a spicy barbecue dish or cold entrée.

PEEL CUCUMBERS, cut in half lengthwise and run a spoon down the center to remove seeds. Chop into ½-inch (1-cm) pieces. Combine in a large bowl with tomatoes, onion, basil and cheese. Refrigerate until ready to serve.

Heat wine, vinegar, sugar and salt in a small saucepan over low heat until sugar dissolves. Set aside to cool. Whisk in oil and season to taste with salt and pepper. Pour dressing over salad and toss until evenly coated. Serve immediately.

Negroni

¾ oz Campari

¾ oz sweet vermouth

¾ oz gin

COMBINE CAMPARI, vermouth and gin in an old-fashioned glass filled with ice. Garnish with an orange twist, if desired.

2 large field cucumbers

3 large tomatoes, seeded and coarsely chopped

½ red onion, thinly sliced

½ cup (125 mL) basil, roughly chopped

1 lb (500 g) bocconcini cheese, torn into bite-size pieces

⅓ cup (75 mL) Valpolicella or Cabernet Franc

3 Tbsp (45 mL) balsamic vinegar

1 Tbsp (15 mL) granulated sugar

1 tsp (5 mL) salt

3 Tbsp (45 mL) extra virgin olive oil

Salt

Freshly ground black pepper

MAKES 6 SERVINGS

Mixed Greens *with* Chambord Vinaigrette

2 Tbsp (25 mL) extra
virgin olive oil

2 Tbsp (25 mL)
red wine vinegar

2 Tbsp (25 mL) Chambord

1 tsp (5 mL) Dijon mustard

Pinch salt

Pinch freshly
ground black pepper

½ lb (250 g) mixed greens, rinsed
and dried

1 red bell pepper, thinly sliced

6 oz (175 g) goat cheese,
crumbled

MAKES 6 SERVINGS

What happens when you take a traditional vinaigrette to the bar? You end up with a salad that gives its number to just about anyone. No worries, this feisty little devil can take care of itself.

WHISK TOGETHER OLIVE OIL, vinegar, Chambord, mustard and salt and pepper. Set aside. Place a handful of greens on salad plates, top with bell pepper and goat cheese. Spoon over vinaigrette and serve immediately.

Raspberry Kamikaze

1½ oz raspberry vodka

½ oz Cointreau

½ oz fresh lime juice

4 oz soda

COMBINE VODKA, Cointreau and lime juice in an old-fashioned glass filled with ice and top with soda. Garnish with a couple of fresh raspberries and a lime wedge, if desired.

Roasted Tomato and Goat Cheese Bruschetta

Roasting tomatoes may seem unnecessarily time consuming, but this is the best bruschetta in the universe. Plum tomatoes work best because they are meatier and have a lower water content than their round counterparts. While they roast, make yourself a G&T (or 3) and relax—you can't rush perfection.

PREHEAT OVEN TO 450°F (230°C).

Toss tomatoes in oil and place sliced-side up in a roasting pan. Combine garlic, shallots, port, vinegar, herbs and salt and pepper. Spoon mixture over tomatoes and roast for 30 to 35 minutes or until tomatoes are browned and tender. Meanwhile, toast baguette slices. Spread each with ½ oz (15 g) goat cheese and top with 2 roasted tomato halves.

Gin and Tonic

1½ oz gin

5 oz tonic

1 slice English cucumber

MIX GIN AND TONIC in an old-fashioned glass filled with ice and garnish with a cucumber slice.

8 plum tomatoes,
cut in half lengthwise

3 Tbsp (45 mL) extra
virgin olive oil

3 cloves garlic, minced

2 shallots, minced

3 Tbsp (45 mL) port

1 Tbsp (15 mL) balsamic vinegar

1 tsp (5 mL) dried basil

1 tsp (5 mL) dried oregano

1½ tsp (7 mL) salt

½ tsp (2 mL) freshly
ground black pepper

8 slices baguette

4 oz (125 g) soft goat cheese

MAKES 8 PIECES

Southern Comfort Baked Beans

3 cups (750 mL) navy beans

6 strips bacon, chopped

1 28-oz (796-mL) can chopped tomatoes

1 large onion, chopped

¾ cup (175 mL) ketchup

¾ cup (175 mL) fancy molasses

½ cup (125 mL) Southern Comfort or bourbon

1 Tbsp (15 mL) dried mustard

½ tsp (2 mL) salt

¼ tsp (1 mL) freshly ground black pepper

Dash hot pepper sauce

MAKES 6 SERVINGS

If you think you don't like baked beans it's because you've never tried them like this. They're perfect with a summer barbecue of chicken and ribs, or served alongside scrambled eggs and breakfast sausage on a Saturday morning. Nothing says lovin' like beans from the oven—although they take all day to cook, so prepare your menu in advance!

RINSE BEANS under cold water, discarding any blemished ones. Place beans in large stockpot and fill with cold water. Bring to a boil and cook for 2 minutes. Remove from heat, cover and let stand for 1 hour. Drain, discarding liquid.

Cover beans with fresh cold water and return to stove. Bring to a boil and simmer for 40 to 50 minutes or until tender. Drain, reserving 1½ cups (375 mL) cooking liquid.

Preheat oven to 300°F (150°C).

Combine beans, tomatoes with juice, bacon, onion, ketchup, molasses, Southern Comfort, dried mustard, salt, pepper, hot pepper sauce and reserved cooking liquid in ovenproof dish, cover and bake for 2½ hours. Uncover and bake for 1 to 2 hours longer or until sauce is thickened and beans are cooked through.

57 Chevy

¾ oz Southern Comfort

¾ oz gin

1 oz orange juice

1 oz pineapple juice

Dash grenadine

COMBINE LIQUEUR, gin, orange juice, pineapple juice and grenadine in cocktail shaker filled with ice and shake vigorously. Strain into an old-fashioned glass filled with ice and garnish with a cherry, if desired.

PASTA AND RISOTTO

Say Cheese

The residents of Parma and Reggio Emilia, Italy, where Parmesan cheese was first made, would rise up in revolt if they knew what passed as their signature product in many of our supermarkets. They take their cheese seriously and have independent inspectors sample and verify internal and external appearance, texture, smell and taste.

The Real Thing

Parmigiano-Reggiano is a part-skim milk cheese with a long aging period—anywhere from 1 to 4 years. During aging, it darkens from a pale yellow to a deep straw color and forms a natural rind. It should be rich, fruity and flaky, not salty, acidic or dry, and should be enjoyed on its own as well as in dishes.

Chicken Fusilli in Pesto Cream

Attack a big bowl of this pasta while watching the news, your favorite soaps, Survivor Kung-Pow *or* Superbowl MCXXVII. *The ingredients can be changed as you like—toss in some sun-dried tomatoes, pancetta or artichoke hearts. The only thing you can't touch is the wine, unless you're pouring yourself a glass, of course.*

PREHEAT OVEN TO 450°F (230°C).

Brush chicken breasts with 1 Tbsp (15 mL) olive oil and season with salt and pepper. Bake for 20 minutes or until chicken is cooked through. Let cool then slice and set aside.

Heat remaining olive oil in a large skillet over medium heat. Sauté onion until tender and translucent. Stir in garlic, butter and mushrooms and sauté until soft and fragrant, about 1 minute. Season with salt and pepper and add wine. Simmer for 5 minutes. Stir in cream and Parmesan cheese and cook until melted. Add pesto and simmer for 5 minutes. Dissolve flour in water, then stir in. Add tomatoes and chicken and cook for 4 minutes or until chicken is heated through.

Meanwhile, bring a large pot of lightly salted water to a boil. Add pasta and cook for 10 to 12 minutes or until *al dente*. Drain and toss with sauce until evenly coated and serve.

Pinot Gris

THIS DISH IS PERFECTLY SUITED to a refreshing white wine such as a Pinot Gris with its clean taste and fruit hints. Remember, the colder you serve your wine the less flavor it has, so take it out of the refrigerator 20 minutes before serving.

3 boneless, skinless chicken breasts

3 Tbsp (45 mL) extra virgin olive oil

Salt

Freshly ground black pepper

1 onion, chopped

3 cloves garlic, minced

2 Tbsp (25 mL) butter

1½ cups (375 mL) sliced button mushrooms

¾ cup (175 mL) Pinot Gris or Chardonnay

½ cup (125 mL) heavy cream (38%)

1 cup (250 mL) grated Parmesan cheese

¾ cup (175 mL) pesto

1 Tbsp (15 mL) all-purpose flour

3 Tbsp (45 mL) water

2 plum tomatoes, diced

2 cups (500 mL) fusilli pasta

MAKES 6 SERVINGS

Scotch-Smoked Salmon Penne

½ lb (250 g) thin-sliced
smoked salmon,
torn into small pieces

¼ cup (50 mL)
single malt scotch

2 Tbsp (25 mL) extra
virgin olive oil

2 shallots, minced

1 cup (250 mL) vegetable
or chicken stock

1 cup (250 mL) Chardonnay

12 oz (350 g) penne

2 cups (500 mL)
heavy cream (38%)

1 Tbsp (15 mL) cornstarch

½ cup (125 mL) grated
Parmesan cheese

¼ cup (50 mL) chopped chives

Freshly ground black pepper

MAKES 4 SERVINGS

This version doesn't stay entirely faithful to convention—traditionally, scotch-smoked salmon uses scotch in the curing process, but it can be difficult to find outside Europe. We suggest foregoing the hunt for the genuine article. Instead, try using a nice peaty Highland-Island single malt scotch to bring out the best in the salmon. If you need more flavor, chew on a cigar. (See page 166 for Scotch 101.)

LINE THE BOTTOM of a small casserole dish with smoked salmon. Pour scotch over salmon, cover dish with plastic wrap and marinate at room temperature for about 1 hour.

Heat 1 Tbsp (15 mL) olive oil in a large skillet over medium heat. Cook shallots until translucent and beginning to brown. Add stock and wine, bring to a boil and cook for 2 to 3 minutes.

Meanwhile, cook pasta according to package instructions.

Slowly stir cream into stock mixture. Dissolve cornstarch in 1 Tbsp (15 mL) water and stir into sauce. Add Parmesan cheese and simmer until thickened, being careful not to boil. Remove from heat and stir in smoked salmon and chives.

Serve sauce over pasta and garnish with fresh pepper, remaining chives or grated Parmesan.

Pink Lemonade

1½ oz scotch

5 oz lemonade

Splash cranberry juice

COMBINE SCOTCH, lemonade and cranberry juice in an ice-filled Collins glass and garnish with a lemon twist, if desired.

GREAT SCOT

Scotland has a long history of smoking salmon, and scotch is often used in the process. In fact, some smoked salmon producers use wood shavings from sherry or scotch casks while curing. The term "nova," used to describe salmon that has been wet cured and smoked, refers to Nova Scotia salmon and the Scottish influence on the smoking and curing process. Lox, from the German "*lachs*," refers to cured, un-smoked salmon. Nova tends to offer a less salty and more refined taste.

Killer Pasta

Have fun with your pasta and try some of the 400 available varieties, like strozzapretti or "strangled priest," for example. Like many things in old-world Europe each pasta shape has its own lineage, region and purpose.

Fresh pasta is always best but some more specialized shapes may only be available in dry form. When cooking pasta follow the package instructions and don't rinse unless instructed to do so. Different types of pasta work better with different types of sauces.

Long cut

Long-cut pasta is generally best suited for heavy and chunky sauces. Ribbons such as linguini or fettuccini and rods like spaghetti are long cut.

Short cut

Short-cut pasta tends to hold sauce well and is ideal for light or cream-based sauces. Penne, rigatoni or ear-shaped orecchiette are short cut.

Tagliatelle

Ideal for pesto and light fish or meat sauces, tagliatelle creates nests of pasta, inspired by hairdos from the Italian Renaissance.

Soup

Small, typically dense pastas, such as stelline (little stars) and farfalline (little butterflies), are ideal for mixing with stock to make hearty soups.

Filled

Tortellini and ravioli stuffed with various meats, cheeses or herbs are suited to most sauces.

Fettuccine *with* Leek Pesto and Sambuca Cream

LEEK PESTO

¼ cup (50 mL) pine nuts

¼ cup + 2 Tbsp (75 mL) extra virgin olive oil

¼ cup (50 mL) grated Parmesan cheese

¼ cup (50 mL) ground almonds

¼ cup (50 mL) fresh parsley

4 cloves garlic

2 cups (500 mL) sliced leeks (white part only)

PASTA

1½ cups (375 mL) sliced cherry tomatoes

3 boneless, skinless chicken breasts

1 cup (250 mL) heavy cream (38 %)

1 cup (250 mL) milk

2 Tbsp (25 mL) fresh lemon juice

½ cup (125 mL) white sambuca

1 tsp (5 mL) salt

1 lb (500 g) fettuccine

MAKES 6 SERVINGS

The leek pesto can be frozen for up to 3 months, making this an ideal meal-on-the-go. The richness of the sambuca and cream is tempered by the savory leeks and acidic tomatoes. As with any pasta, feel free to add your favorite ingredient or seasonal vegetable.

TO MAKE PESTO, toast pine nuts in 1 Tbsp (15 mL) olive oil over medium heat in skillet until lightly browned, about 5 minutes. Pay attention—they burn easily. Remove from heat and allow to cool.

Combine ¼ cup (50 mL) olive oil, Parmesan, almonds, parsley, garlic, leeks and pine nuts in food processor or blender and purée. Set aside until ready to use.

Preheat oven to 450°F (230°C).

Roast cherry tomatoes on a lightly oiled baking sheet for 20 to 25 minutes, or until soft. Remove from oven and set aside.

Heat remaining 1 Tbsp (15 mL) olive oil in a large skillet over medium heat and sauté chicken breasts until juices run clear, about 8 to 10 minutes per side. Remove chicken from skillet, allow to cool, and slice diagonally into thin strips. Add pesto to pan then slowly add cream and milk, stirring constantly. Add lemon juice, sambuca and salt. Bring to a simmer, reduce heat to low and allow to thicken until sauce coats the back of a spoon, about 15 minutes.

Meanwhile, bring a large pot of lightly salted water to a boil. Add pasta and cook for 10 to 12 minutes or until *al dente*. Drain.

Toss chicken and tomatoes with sambuca cream and serve over fettuccine.

Elderflower Fizz

1 oz vodka

1 oz elderflower cordial

6 oz soda

COMBINE VODKA, cordial and soda in an ice-filled Collins glass and garnish with an orange wheel, if desired.

Champagne and French Herb Risotto

Fresh herbs, fresh herbs, fresh herbs—there's no substitute. In this dish, dried herbs simply can't compete. The difference is like comparing a natural summer tan against one that came from the drugstore. The combination below is a great guideline, but add as many different herbs as you like. Toss in some mint leaves to liven things up or a few sage leaves to evoke that comfort food feeling.

BRING STOCK TO A SIMMER in a saucepan, then reduce heat, but keep hot.

Melt butter and oil together in a large stockpot over medium heat. Add shallots and cook for 1 to 2 minutes, or until softened. Add garlic and cook for an additional minute. Add rice and stir with a wooden spoon until each grain of rice is coated with butter. Pour in champagne and stir until it has been absorbed. Add a ladle of stock and stir until it has been absorbed. Continue this process, adding a ladle at a time, until all of the liquid has been absorbed and the rice is tender but firm, about 18 to 20 minutes.

Coarsely chop herbs and toss them into the pot with Parmesan cheese and cream. Season with salt and pepper. Remove from heat, cover and let stand 2 minutes. Spoon into warmed bowls and garnish with a sprig of rosemary.

Rosemary Martini

3 oz vodka

Dash dry vermouth

Sprig rosemary

COMBINE VODKA, vermouth and rosemary in a cocktail shaker filled with ice and shake vigorously. Strain into a chilled martini glass and garnish with another sprig of rosemary, if desired.

4 cups (1 L) vegetable stock

¼ cup (50 mL) butter

1 Tbsp (15 mL) extra virgin olive oil

8 shallots, finely chopped

2 garlic cloves, minced

1½ cups (375 mL) risotto rice

⅓ cup (75 mL) champagne

½ cup (125 mL) fresh herbs, such as thyme, rosemary, oregano, savory, marjoram or a combination

1½ cups (375 mL) grated Parmesan cheese

2 Tbsp (25 mL) light cream (18%)

Salt

Freshly ground black pepper

MAKES 4 SERVINGS

RICE TRY

Selecting good quality rice is critical to making grade-A risotto. Any of three types of short-grained rice can be used—arborio, carnaroli or vialone nano. Short-grained rice absorbs a large amount of liquid without losing its texture. Arborio is the most common type and produces an intense risotto, but it can become stiff if overcooked. Carnaroli is a more expensive rice but tends to be less susceptible to overcooking. Vialone nano is the favorite of Venetian cooks and creates a luscious, ultra-creamy risotto.

Lemon and Fennel Risotto

This vegetarian risotto is great on its own or as a sophisticated accompaniment to Mojo Pork Tenderloin (page 108) or Beer Can Chicken (page 105). Substitute the vegetable stock for chicken stock if you're planning to serve it with meat, making it slightly less than vegetarian. We'd also like to suggest that a side of steamed fresh green beans dripping in butter and freshly ground black pepper might just bring this meal into the realm of the super-fantastic.

REMOVE FRONDS FROM FENNEL and chop coarsely. Set aside. Remove hard green stems from fennel, cut bulb in half lengthwise and slice thinly. Set aside.

Bring stock to a simmer in a saucepan, then reduce heat to keep warm.

Melt butter and oil together in a large stockpot over medium heat. Add shallots and cook for 1 to 2 minutes, or until softened. Add sliced fennel and lemon zest and cook for an additional 2 to 3 minutes. Add rice and stir with a wooden spoon until each grain is coated with butter. Pour in vodka and wine and stir until absorbed. Add a ladle of stock and stir until absorbed. Continue this process, adding a ladle at a time, until all of the liquid has been absorbed and the rice is tender but firm, about 18 to 20 minutes.

Stir in Parmesan cheese and cream and season to taste with salt and pepper. Remove from heat, cover and let stand 2 minutes. Spoon into warmed bowls and garnish with chopped fennel fronds.

Citrus Fizz

1 tsp (5 mL) granulated sugar

1¾ oz lemon vodka

Dash Pernod

Soda

DISSOLVE SUGAR with vodka and pernod in a Collins glass. Fill with ice and top with soda. Garnish with a lemon wedge, if desired.

1 bulb fennel with green fronds

4 cups (1 L) vegetable or chicken stock

¼ cup (50 mL) butter

1 Tbsp (15 mL) extra virgin olive oil

8 shallots, finely chopped

2 tsp (10 mL) grated lemon zest

1½ cups (375 mL) risotto rice (see page 77)

¼ cup (50 mL) lemon vodka

¼ cup (50 mL) Soave or Pinot Gris

1½ cups (375 mL) grated Parmesan cheese

2 Tbsp (25 mL) light cream (18%)

Salt

Freshly ground black pepper

MAKES 4 SERVINGS

Beer-Poached Sausage Jambalaya

2 12-oz (341-mL) bottles dark ale

4 chorizo sausages

1 Tbsp (15 mL) vegetable oil

3 boneless, skinless chicken breasts, cut into 1-inch (2.5-cm) cubes

4 cloves garlic, minced

2 stalks celery, chopped

2 onions, chopped

1 red bell pepper, chopped

1 green bell pepper, chopped

1½ cups (375 mL) chicken stock

2 cups (500 mL) instant rice

2 bay leaves

1½ tsp (7 mL) chili powder

1½ tsp (7 mL) dried thyme

1½ tsp (7 mL) dried oregano

½ tsp (2 mL) salt

½ tsp (2 mL) freshly ground black pepper

¼ tsp (1 mL) hot pepper flakes

1 28-oz (796-mL) can chopped tomatoes

12 oz (350 g) large shrimp (21–30 count), peeled and deveined

MAKES 6 SERVINGS

New Orleans fuses French and southern American cuisine to create something totally unique. Of course, we can't leave well enough alone, so we've added our two cents (or, more accurately, 24 oz) to this dish.

BRING BEER TO A SIMMER in a large skillet over medium heat. Pierce sausages with a fork and add to beer. Cover and poach sausages for 8 minutes. Remove from pan, allow to cool and slice diagonally. Set aside. Save poaching liquid.

Heat oil in a large stockpot over medium-high heat, add chicken and sauté for 3 minutes. Add sausage and cook until chicken browns lightly, about 4 minutes. Remove from pot and set aside. Add garlic, celery, onion and peppers and sauté until onion becomes translucent. Deglaze with chicken stock and 1 cup (250 mL) of poaching liquid. Add rice, herbs and spices. Stir in sausage, chicken and tomatoes. Reduce heat and simmer for 20 to 25 minutes or until almost all the liquid is absorbed. Stir in shrimp and cook for an additional 5 minutes, or until shrimp are bright pink and cooked through.

Sazerac

Reputed to be the world's first cocktail, the Sazerac is believed to have been invented in New Orleans in the 1790s by apothecary Antoine Peychaud and was intended for medicinal purposes. Here's your prescription.

½ oz Pernod

1 sugar cube

Angostura Bitters

1½ oz bourbon

Lemon twist

RINSE AN OLD-FASHIONED GLASS with Pernod then discard Pernod. Put sugar in glass and saturate with bitters, add ice cubes and bourbon, and garnish with a twist of lemon.

Rémy Martin Risotto

½ cup (125 mL) butter

1 cup (250 mL) finely sliced
cremini mushrooms

2 Tbsp (25 mL) Rémy Martin
or other cognac

1 tsp (5 mL) salt

½ tsp (2 mL) freshly
ground black pepper

¼ cup (50 mL)
light cream (18%)

4 cups (1 L) vegetable stock

1 Tbsp (15 mL) extra
virgin olive oil

8 shallots, finely chopped

2 garlic cloves, minced

1½ cups (375 mL) risotto rice
(see page 77)

1½ cups (375 mL) grated
Parmesan cheese

½ cup (125 mL)
chopped Italian parsley

MAKES 4 SERVINGS

Risotto is a lot like your old college roommate—it needs constant attention or risks turning into a hard and bitter mess. Pour yourself a stiff Rusty Nail when you begin so that your left hand has something to do while you stir with your right.

HEAT ¼ CUP (50 ML) BUTTER in a skillet until foaming. Add mushrooms and cook for 5 minutes or until soft. Add cognac, salt and pepper and simmer until reduced by half, then stir in cream. Simmer for 5 minutes, until sauce has thickened slightly. Set aside.

Put stock in a saucepan and heat until almost boiling then reduce heat until barely simmering to keep warm.

Heat remaining butter and oil in a deep skillet or stockpot over medium heat. Add shallots and cook for 1 to 2 minutes until softened but not browned. Add garlic and cook for 1 minute.

Add rice and stir until each grain is coated with butter. Add a ladle of stock and stir until liquid has been absorbed. Continue this process, adding stock a ladle at a time, until all of the liquid has been absorbed and the rice is tender but firm, about 18 to 20 minutes.

Add reserved mushroom mixture, Parmesan cheese and parsley and season to taste with salt and pepper. Mix well. Remove from heat, cover and let stand for 2 minutes. Spoon into warmed bowls and top with extra Parmesan cheese shavings and a sprig of parsley, if desired.

Rusty Nail

1½ oz scotch

¾ oz Drambuie

COMBINE INGREDIENTS in an old-fashioned glass with a couple of ice cubes and garnish with a maraschino cherry, if desired.

ENTRÉES

Chicken Molé *Shandy Town* 84

Roasted Turkey Breast with Cranberry-Pear Chutney
Simply Grand 85

Cornish Hens with Dried Cherry and Hazelnut Stuffing
Fruit 'n' Nut 87

Stuffed Pork with Blackberry Wine Jus *Fred and Ginger* 88

Pork Tenderloin with Peaches and Ginger
Peach Spritzer 90

Coffee Porter Sunday Roast *Espresso Especial* 91

Thai Orange-Basil Beef *Sexy Bitch* 92

Braised Lamb Shanks with Sherry-Poached Figs
The All-Nighter 93

Roast Rack of Lamb with Rosemary and Jägermeister
Deer in the Headlights 95

Canadian Club and Maple-Glazed Salmon *Manhattan* 96

Pumpkin and Coconut Curry *La Palapa* 99

Red Snapper in Banana Curry *Banana Daiquiri* 100

Beeritos *Classic Margarita* 101

Beer Crust Pizza *Boilemaker* 102

COOKING WITH BOOZE

Chicken Molé

1 Tbsp (15 mL) vegetable oil

6 boneless, skinless
chicken breasts, cut into pieces

2 12-oz (341-mL) bottles
dark lager

½ cup (125 mL) fancy molasses

½ cup (125 mL) chopped onion

1 Tbsp (15 mL) minced
jalapeño pepper,
seeds removed

2 garlic cloves, minced

1 tsp (5 mL) ground cinnamon

¾ tsp (4 mL) chili powder

¼ tsp (1 mL) ground cumin

Pinch ground cloves

Pinch ground cardamom

3 Tbsp (45 mL) smooth
peanut butter

2 oz (50 g) semisweet
chocolate, chopped

2 Tbsp (25 mL) butter

2 Tbsp (25 mL) toasted
sesame seeds

MAKES 6 SERVINGS

Olé molé! Mexico's diverse molés are as spectacular as the molé on your aunt's chin. They range from simple guacamole to more complex sauces containing flavors rarely used in savory Western cooking. This hearty hombre includes chocolate, peanut butter and cinnamon and can take down a hungry crowd with enough left over to feed the neighbors.

HEAT OIL IN LARGE SKILLET over medium-high heat. Add chicken and cook until browned on all sides, about 8 to 10 minutes. Add half a bottle of beer and ¼ cup (50 mL) molasses and simmer until chicken is cooked and sauce is slightly thickened, about 10 minutes. Remove from skillet and set aside.

Reduce heat to medium and to same skillet add onion, jalapeño and garlic. Cook for 3 minutes or until tender. Add cinnamon, chili powder, cumin, cloves, cardamom, 1 bottle of beer, peanut butter and remaining molasses. Remove from heat and blend ingredients in food processor or blender until smooth. Return mixture to skillet, add chocolate, butter and remaining beer. Cook until thickened, about 5 minutes. Add chicken pieces and heat until warmed through. Serve over rice and sprinkle with sesame seeds.

Shandy Town

8 oz ginger ale

8 oz dark lager

Slice lime

FILL A PILSNER GLASS with ginger ale and top with lager. Garnish with lime.

Roasted Turkey Breast *with* Cranberry-Pear Chutney

Turkey, that long-standing seasonal favorite, gets a makeover with this bright, savory chutney. Packaged turkey breasts are available in most grocery stores, which makes this recipe an instant comfort-food classic. All the love of the holiday season—and none of the family. Perfect.

PREHEAT OVEN TO 350°F (180°C).

Place turkey breast on rack in shallow roasting pan, brush with olive oil and sprinkle with salt. Toss sage and thyme together, spread evenly under turkey skin and sprinkle any remaining over surface. Loosely tent with aluminum foil and roast 1 hour. Remove foil, add water to cover bottom of pan and roast for an additional 30 minutes, or until internal temperature reaches 170°F (75°C) on a meat thermometer. Baste occasionally.

Remove turkey from oven, tent with foil and let stand for 10 minutes before carving. Serve with Cranberry-Pear Chutney.

To make the chutney, combine cranberries, pears, onion, brown sugar, vinegar, brandy, ginger, orange rind, pepper flakes, mustard seeds and salt in a medium saucepan over medium-low heat, stirring occasionally for about 30 minutes or until berries burst and pears are tender. Remove from heat, cool and serve with turkey breasts. Will keep refrigerated for up to a month.

Simply Grand

1½ oz Grand Marnier

2 oz orange juice

2 oz cranberry juice

COMBINE GRAND MARNIER, orange juice and cranberry juice in an old-fashioned glass filled with ice and garnish with a fresh cranberry, if desired.

TURKEY

3½–4½ lb (1.75–2 kg) turkey breast, skin on

2 Tbsp (25 mL) extra virgin olive oil

1 tsp (5 mL) salt

2 Tbsp (25 mL) chopped fresh sage

2 Tbsp (25 mL) chopped fresh thyme

CRANBERRY-PEAR CHUTNEY

1 cup (250 mL) fresh cranberries

4 firm pears, peeled and diced

1 cup (250 mL) minced onion

½ cup (125 mL) packed brown sugar

½ cup (125 mL) cider vinegar

½ cup (125 mL) apricot brandy

1 Tbsp (15 mL) grated fresh ginger

2 tsp (10 mL) grated orange rind

½ tsp (2 mL) hot pepper flakes

1 tsp (5 mL) white mustard seeds

Pinch salt

MAKES 4 SERVINGS

Cornish Hens *with* Dried Cherry and Hazelnut Stuffing

Having the boss over for dinner? Trying to impress the unimpressible in-laws? Need to apologize without admitting guilt? Cornish hens selflessly sacrifice their tiny, meaningless lives in service of the ultimate suck-up dish. If you want something less finicky you can substitute a roasting chicken and increase cooking time to 2 to 3 hours, depending on size.

PREHEAT OVEN TO 400°F (200°C).

Crisp bacon in a large skillet over medium heat. Drain on paper towel, crumble and set aside. Sauté onion and celery in bacon renderings until soft, about 10 minutes. Stir in 1 Tbsp (15 mL) thyme, sage, hazelnuts and Frangelico. Pour onion mixture over chopped bread and toss well. Drizzle with chicken stock and toss to combine. Stir in crumbled bacon, cherries, ½ tsp (2 mL) salt and 1 tsp (5 mL) pepper. Set aside.

Wash hens and pat dry. Spoon stuffing mixture into cavities. Combine softened butter, remaining thyme, ½ tsp (2 mL) salt and 1 tsp (5 mL) pepper. Rub hens with butter mixture and place on rack in large roasting pan. Roast for 45 minutes to 1 hour or until internal temperature reaches 170°F (75°C). Remove from oven and tent with aluminum foil. Let rest 10 minutes before serving.

Fruit 'n' Nut

1½ oz Frangelico

8 oz cranberry juice

FILL A COLLINS GLASS with ice, add Frangelico and top with cranberry juice. Garnish with an orange wheel and a couple fresh cranberries, if desired.

3 slices bacon

1 large onion, chopped

3 stalks celery, chopped

2 Tbsp (25 mL) chopped fresh thyme

1 tsp (5 mL) chopped fresh sage

1 cup (250 mL) blanched and chopped hazelnuts

2 Tbsp (25 mL) Frangelico liqueur

4 cups (1 L) chopped stale bread

½ cup (125 mL) chicken stock

½ cup (125 mL) dried cherries

1 tsp (5 mL) salt

2 tsp (10 mL) freshly ground black pepper

6 Cornish hens
(about 1 lb/500 g each)

6 Tbsp (90 mL) butter, softened

MAKES 6 SERVINGS

Stuffed Pork *with* Blackberry Wine Jus

2 pork tenderloins
(¾ lb/375 g each)

½ lb (250 g) soft goat cheese

2½ cups (625 mL) fresh spinach

2 cloves garlic, minced

4 roasted
red peppers, quartered
(see sidebar page 58)

Freshly ground black pepper

1 Tbsp (15 mL) butter

1 shallot, minced

2 cups (500 mL) blackberry wine

1 Tbsp (15 mL) fresh lemon juice

1 tsp (5 mL) salt

1 Tbsp (15 mL) cornstarch

MAKES 4–6 SERVINGS

LIQUOR LAB

The liquor companies, in their selfless quest to provide consumers with new and innovative products, are rolling out the fruits of their most recent foray. Over the past few years we've seen a number of fruit- or spice-infused vodkas and now, quick on their heels, are flavored rums and gins. This opens a Pandora's Box of experimentation, so run (in an orderly fashion) to your local liquor store. Pick up a bottle of citrus rum or gin and experiment with it in your favorite cocktail or recipe. It's a great excuse to don a lab coat and lock yourself in the basement, all in the name of science, of course.

This recipe uses the delicate sweetness of a blackberry-flavored wine to transform a typical jus. The jus is a vibrant contrast to the savory goat cheese and earthy spinach, making this a roast to remember. Allow it to sit for at least 10 minutes before attempting to carve to help keep all the layers together. Use a very sharp knife and slice thickly.

BUTTERFLY TENDERLOINS by slicing them lengthwise along the center but not all the way through, leaving about ½ inch (1 cm) thickness. Flip 1 tenderloin over and slice lengthwise again on either side of the center cut, making a "W" pattern. Cover with plastic wrap and pound with meat mallet until about ½–¾ inch (1–2 cm) thick or until all your pent-up familial aggression is freed. Repeat with second tenderloin. Overlay the edges of the 2 tenderloins, then use mallet to flatten them to help them stay together.

Preheat oven to 375°F (190°C).

Break up goat cheese and divide across tenderloins, press in spinach and add garlic and roasted peppers. Cover again with plastic wrap and gently mallet everything into place. Roll up lengthwise, like a Swiss roll, and tie with butcher's twine—remember you can't over-tie! Season to taste with freshly ground black pepper.

Roast pork for about 40 minutes or until internal temperature reaches 150°F (65°C). Tent meat in aluminum foil to rest for 10 minutes before carving. Reserve any juices.

Meanwhile, melt butter in a large skillet over medium heat. Add shallot and sauté until translucent. Add wine, lemon juice, salt and reserved pan juices. Dissolve cornstarch in 2 Tbsp (25 mL) water and add to pan. Bring mixture to a boil, lower heat and simmer until sauce is slightly thickened. Strain if required. Carve pork and serve with sauce.

Fred and Ginger

1 oz Calvados

4 oz ginger ale

Splash orange juice

COMBINE CALVADOS, ginger ale and orange juice in an old-fashioned glass filled with ice and garnish with an orange wheel, if desired.

Pork Tenderloin *with* Peaches and Ginger

6 sprigs fresh thyme, plus extra for garnish

4 cloves garlic, sliced

2 pork tenderloins (¾ lb/375 g each)

1 tsp (5 mL) salt

1 tsp (5 mL) freshly ground black pepper

1½ cups (375 mL) late harvest Riesling

2 Tbsp (25 mL) apple cider vinegar

6 large peaches

2 Tbsp (25 mL) extra virgin olive oil

1 Tbsp (15 mL) butter

1 Tbsp (15 mL) minced fresh ginger

1 Tbsp (15 mL) honey

Pinch hot pepper flakes

MAKES 6 SERVINGS

There's nothing like biting into a fresh, locally grown peach. Combine that great flavor with the sweet acidity of late harvest Riesling and the bite of fresh ginger, and this meal becomes almost a religious experience—perfect for Sunday dinner.

SANDWICH THYME and garlic between tenderloins, tie together with butcher's twine and place in 9- × 13-inch (23- × 33-cm) baking dish. Combine salt, pepper, 1 cup (250 mL) wine and vinegar in a small bowl and pour over pork. Cover and refrigerate for 3 hours.

Blanch peaches in boiling water for 30 seconds, remove and place in a bowl of ice water. Peel skin from peaches and slice into sections. Set aside.

Preheat oven to 400°F (200°C).

Remove pork from refrigerator and discard marinade. Brush pork with olive oil and place on rack in roasting pan. Roast for 30 to 40 minutes or until internal temperature reaches 150°F (65°C) on a meat thermometer, for medium. Remove from roasting pan and tent with aluminum foil.

Heat butter in medium skillet over medium-high heat until foaming. Add ginger and peach slices and cook until soft, about 3 minutes. Add remaining wine, honey and hot pepper flakes. Reduce over medium heat until liquid is almost completely evaporated.

Remove strings from pork. Slice into medallions and arrange on serving platter. Pour over peaches and garnish with sprigs of thyme.

Peach Spritzer

1 oz peach juice

4 oz Chardonnay

Soda

COMBINE PEACH JUICE and wine in a white wine glass filled with ice and top with soda.

BE KIND TO SWINE

Contrary to popular belief, pork doesn't need to be well done. In fact, ideally, there should be a hint of pink in the center. To ensure maximum juiciness place cooked pork in an aluminum foil tent to rest for 10 minutes. This allows the internal juices to be absorbed back into the pork and not lost on the cutting board when sliced.

Coffee Porter Sunday Roast

1 12-oz (341-mL) bottle
coffee porter

⅓ cup (75 mL) pomegranate
molasses

1 onion, chopped

4 cloves garlic, sliced

1 tsp (5 mL) freshly
ground black pepper

3 lb (1.5 kg) top sirloin beef roast

1½ cups (375 mL) beef stock

2 Tbsp (25 mL) butter, softened

2 Tbsp (25 mL) all-purpose flour

MAKES 6 SERVINGS

The marinade for this roast creates a wonderfully deep and rich gravy that, much like Sunday, is a little bitter and a little sweet. So as you mentally prepare for another week of the grind, know that there's good news on the brown-bag front. Sandwiches made from the leftovers will give you something to look forward to on Monday.

COMBINE BEER, molasses, onion, garlic and pepper. Place roast in deep bowl and pour over marinade. Cover and refrigerate for at least 3 hours, or overnight if possible.

Adjust oven rack to the lower-middle position and heat to 250°F (120°C).

Remove roast from marinade. Pour marinade through a mesh sieve to remove onion and garlic and set aside. Heat oil in a large ovenproof skillet or heavy-duty roasting pan over medium-high heat until smoking. Sear the roast until well browned, about 2 minutes on each side.

Transfer skillet to oven and cook uncovered until internal temperature reaches 110°F (43°C), 45 minutes to 1 hour. Increase the oven to 500°F (260°C) and cook until the internal temperature reaches 120°F (49°C) for rare or 125°F (52°C) for medium-rare, 10 to 20 minutes longer. Transfer to cutting board, tent with aluminum foil and let rest for 15 minutes.

Meanwhile, add marinade and beef stock to pan and bring to a simmer over medium heat, making sure to scrape all the brown bits from the pan. Cream together butter and flour and whisk into beer mixture, a bit at a time, until completely incorporated. Continue whisking for 5 minutes or until gravy has thickened. Strain gravy through mesh sieve to remove any large charred bits. Carve roast into thin slices and serve with gravy.

Espresso Especial

1½ oz vodka

1½ oz espresso (or strong coffee)

1 oz Kahlúa

COMBINE VODKA, espresso and Kahlúa in a cocktail shaker filled with ice. Strain into a chilled martini glass and garnish with espresso bean, if desired.

STRANGE BREW

This recipe has both coffee porter and pomegranate molasses, two things that may not be readily available in every community. Coffee porter is a full-bodied beer, flavored with—you guessed it—coffee. Mill St. Brewery in Toronto makes a wonderful one but if you can't find it near you, add a shot of espresso or strong coffee to a dark beer. Pomegranate molasses can be found in Middle Eastern grocery stores or online, but for a quick substitute you can use equal parts grenadine and fresh lemon juice.

Thai Orange-Basil Beef

1½ lb (750 g) flank steak

3 cloves garlic, minced

½ cup (125 mL) fresh
orange juice

1 Tbsp (15 mL) grated orange zest

3 Tbsp (45 mL) soy sauce

2 tsp (10 mL) grated fresh ginger

2 cups (500 mL)
basmati or jasmine rice

¼ cup (50 mL) vegetable oil

½ cup (125 mL) triple sec

4 small red chilies,
finely chopped

½ cup (125 mL) chopped
fresh basil

2 green onions,
white and green part,
sliced diagonally

MAKES 4 SERVINGS

One of Toronto's best-kept secrets is Salad King. This jewel, surrounded by big-box stores and fast-food franchises, is home to arguably the best Thai food this side of Thailand. This dish was inspired by our friends at Salad King who have served us more meals than we care to count. We wanted to see first-hand how these miracles are performed, but the flying knives, four-foot flames and surgical precision of the operation scared the hell out of us, so we settled for a Singha and a heaping plate of their classic Orange-Basil Beef.

TRIM FLANK STEAK of any excess fat and slice across the grain into ½-inch (1-cm) strips. Place strips in shallow baking dish. Combine garlic, orange juice, zest, soy sauce and ginger and pour half the marinade over steak strips. Cover and refrigerate for at least 3 hours or overnight, if possible. Set aside remaining marinade.

Meanwhile, prepare rice according to package directions and set aside.

Heat oil in a large skillet over medium-high heat and add steak, working in batches, making sure not to overcrowd pan. Cook, stirring constantly until lightly browned, about 8 to 9 minutes.

Add reserved marinade, triple sec, chilies and basil to steak mixture. Cook until slightly thickened, about 1 to 2 minutes. Serve over rice and garnish with green onions.

Sexy Bitch

1 oz peach schnapps

¾ oz triple sec

3 oz orange juice

3 oz cranberry juice

COMBINE SCHNAPPS, triple sec, orange juice and cranberry juice in a Collins glass filled with ice and garnish with a few frozen cranberries, if desired.

Braised Lamb Shanks *with* Sherry-Poached Figs

Lamb makes any occasion special, and for those of us who grew up eating lamb, the rich aroma immediately conjures up memories of Easter dinners. Sticky figs, rich with honey, and sherry provide a sugary contrast to the earthy meat. Serve this dish with some fava beans and a nice Chianti.

FOR THE FIGS, bring honey, sherry and ¼ cup (50 mL) water to a gentle simmer in a small saucepan over low heat. Reduce mixture by half, stirring constantly. Add figs and cook for about 1 minute. Remove from heat and set aside.

Preheat oven to 400°F (200°C).

Heat oil and butter in a large skillet over medium-high heat and sear lamb shanks on both sides. Reserve any pan juices. Transfer seared lamb to a roasting pan. Add bay leaf, celery, carrots and onions. Bake for 20 minutes. Remove from oven and season with salt and pepper to taste, garlic, rosemary, thyme, wine, tomato paste and both stocks.

Reduce oven temperature to 350°F (180°C). Cover with a tight-fitting lid or aluminum foil and braise until tender, about 1 hour. Remove from oven and tent with aluminum foil for 10 minutes.

Add reserved pan juices to roasting pan and skim off excess fat with a spoon or gravy separator. Strain mixture through a fine mesh sieve into a medium saucepan and bring to a simmer over low heat. Season to taste. Serve lamb shanks in pan jus with figs on the side.

The All-Nighter

1½ oz gin

½ oz fresh lemon juice

5 oz raspberry juice

COMBINE GIN, lemon juice and raspberry juice in an old-fashioned glass filled with ice and garnish with a few fresh raspberries, if desired.

SHERRY-POACHED FIGS

½ cup (125 mL) honey

½ cup (125 mL) sherry

8 fresh figs, quartered

LAMB

¼ cup (50 mL) vegetable oil

¼ cup (50 mL) butter

4 lamb shanks (about 3 lb/1.5 kg in total)

1 bay leaf

2 celery stalks, diced

2 small carrots, peeled and sliced

2 medium onions, sliced

Salt

Freshly ground black pepper

4 cloves garlic, minced

1 tsp (5 mL) chopped rosemary

1 tsp (5 mL) chopped thyme

1 cup (250 mL) Cabernet Sauvignon or Bordeaux

¼ cup (50 mL) tomato paste

3 cups (750 mL) beef stock

3 cups (750 mL) chicken stock

MAKES 4 SERVINGS

HOT LEGS

For the best presentation expose the tip of the lamb shank bone during the cooking process by slicing around the lamb shank about an inch (2.5 cm) from the tip.

LAMB, HOGGET AND MUTTON

Our ovine friends are best consumed as lamb, under 1 year old, and before they become hogget. Hogget is the ovine teenager and it's chewier and more intense in flavor than lamb—a result of severe punishment for wrecking the family car. Hogget is best suited to roasting, stewing and braising. After the second messy divorce, hogget becomes mutton—the jaded ovine adult. Mutton has the strongest flavor, typically not favored by the contemporary palate. It requires extended cooking times and is best suited to curing, stewing and braising.

Roast Rack of Lamb *with* Rosemary and Jägermeister

Lamb racks are all about the presentation. Ask your butcher to French your rack to expose the bones. Typically, 1 rack will serve 2 people, although this obviously depends on the size. This impressive dish is best served with pan jus, garlic mashed potatoes and fresh green beans.

PREHEAT OVEN TO 375°F (190°C).

Blend olive oil, rosemary, garlic, Jägermeister and salt and pepper in a food processor or blender. Rub mixture over lamb and place bone-side up in roasting pan. Cover tips of bones loosely with aluminum foil and roast lamb for about 25 minutes or until internal temperature reaches 125°F (50°C) on a meat thermometer for medium-rare, or for 30 to 35 minutes for medium. Remove from heat and tent in aluminum foil.

Meanwhile, deglaze roasting pan with red wine over medium-high heat. Dissolve cornstarch in 1 cup (250 mL) cold water and whisk into roasting pan with butter. Bring to rolling boil for about 1 minute. Strain gravy through a fine mesh sieve and season to taste with salt and pepper. Keep warm.

Carve lamb between bones into chops and serve with gravy.

Deer in the Headlights

1 oz Jägermeister

5 oz cola

COMBINE THE JÄGERMEISTER and cola in an old-fashioned glass filled with ice and garnish with an orange slice, if desired.

¼ cup (50 mL) extra virgin olive oil

¼ cup (50 mL) fresh rosemary

2 garlic cloves

¼ cup (50 mL) Jägermeister

1 Tbsp (15 mL) salt

2 tsp (10 mL) freshly ground black pepper

2 racks of lamb (1½ lb/750 g each), frenched

¾ cup (175 mL) Cabernet Sauvignon or Shiraz

2 Tbsp (25 mL) cornstarch

1 Tbsp (15 mL) butter

Salt

Freshly ground black pepper

MAKES 4 SERVINGS

GETTING FOND OF DEGLAZING

Deglazing is the process of removing the caramelized bits that remain in the bottom of your pan after sautéing meat or vegetables. These richly flavored bits are called the *fond* and the purpose of deglazing is to reincorporate these flavors into a sauce or dish. To deglaze a pan, keep the pan over heat and remove the sautéed ingredients and any excess fat, leaving only the caramelized fond. Add your deglazing liquid, which is typically stock or wine, and use a wooden spoon to scrape the fond off the bottom of the pan. Voilà—deglazed.

Canadian Club and Maple-Glazed Salmon

2 Tbsp (25 mL) butter

1 clove garlic, minced

½ cup (125 mL) maple syrup (see page 18)

½ cup (125 mL) rye whisky

2 Tbsp (25 mL) fresh lemon juice

4 salmon fillets (1-inch/2.5-cm thick)

8 slices thick-cut bacon

Salt

Freshly ground black pepper

MAKES 4 SERVINGS

Salmon with maple syrup is Canada's unofficial national dish. Truly patriotic Canadians understand that only one thing could make it better—the addition of bacon. We've taken this sticky salmon dish and made it just a little more sophisticated with the addition of a little rye whisky. Put on a hockey sweater, dig your best wooly toque out of the closet and enjoy, eh!

MELT BUTTER OVER LOW HEAT in a medium saucepan. Add garlic, maple syrup, whisky and lemon juice. Bring to a gentle simmer for about 1 minute then remove from heat and set aside.

If desired remove skin from salmon. Wrap each piece of salmon with a slice of bacon. Place salmon in shallow baking dish and marinate with syrup mixture in the refrigerator for 3 hours. Remove and reserve marinade.

Heat just enough vegetable oil to cover the bottom of a large non-stick skillet over medium-high heat. Sear salmon for about 3 minutes per side or until lightly browned. Meanwhile, bring marinade to a boil in a small saucepan over medium heat and simmer for 5 minutes or until slightly thickened. Spoon over steaks and serve.

Manhattan

2 oz rye

¾ oz sweet vermouth

Dash Angostura Bitters

COMBINE RYE, vermouth and bitters in a cocktail shaker filled with ice and shake vigorously. Strain into a chilled martini glass and garnish with a maraschino cherry, if desired.

Pumpkin and Coconut Curry

Pumpkin and coconut work so well together that once you've tried this dish you'll find yourself wanting to sneak the duo into everything—like the movies. This dish is perfect for entertaining on-the-go because cutting up the pumpkin is the most time-consuming part and can easily be done in advance. Butternut or acorn squash are also acceptable substitutes since they tend to be less seasonal than our jack-o'-lantern friend. Canned pumpkin is most definitely not an option for this recipe.

HEAT OIL IN A LARGE SKILLET over medium heat, add shallots and pumpkin and cook until shallots begin to brown. Add coconut rum, chicken broth, coconut milk, sugar, turmeric and fish sauce. Cook until pumpkin is tender, about 8 to 10 minutes.

Meanwhile, prepare rice according to package directions and set aside.

Add cilantro, chilies and shrimp to pumpkin mixture and cook for an additional 5 minutes or until shrimp turns pink and opaque. Serve with rice and garnish with sliced green onions.

La Palapa

2 oz coconut rum

3 oz orange juice

2 oz lemon-lime soda

Splash pineapple juice

COMBINE RUM, orange juice, soda and pineapple juice in a Collins glass filled with ice and garnish with a pineapple wedge, if desired.

2 Tbsp (25 mL) vegetable oil

4 shallots, minced

4 cups (1 L) chopped pumpkin, peeled and seeded (¾-inch/2-cm cubes)

½ cup (125 mL) coconut rum

2 cups (500 mL) chicken stock

1½ cups (375 mL) coconut milk

2 Tbsp (25 mL) granulated sugar

2 tsp (10 mL) turmeric

2 Tbsp (25 mL) fish sauce

2 cups (500 mL) basmati or jasmine rice

1 cup (250 mL) cilantro, chopped

2 small fresh red chilies with seeds, chopped

1 lb (500 g) large shrimp (21–30 count), deveined and tails on

Sliced green onions

MAKES 4–6 SERVINGS

Red Snapper in Banana Curry

3 cloves garlic, minced

¼ cup (50 mL) vegetable oil

½ tsp (2 mL) salt

2 tsp (10 mL) turmeric

1 tsp (5 mL) paprika

1 tsp (5 mL) ground cumin

1 tsp (5 mL) ground cardamom

½ tsp (2 mL) hot pepper flakes

2 tsp (10 mL) fresh lime juice

½ cup (125 mL) crème de banane

1 cup (250 mL)
heavy cream (38%)

4 red snapper fillets
(about 1 lb/500 g total)

¼ cup (50 mL) chopped cilantro

MAKES 4 SERVINGS

If your tax refund bought you a shiny new snow blower instead of a tropical vacation this year, break out the crème de banane and warm things up with this St. Lucia-inspired curry. Better luck next year.

SAUTÉ GARLIC IN 2 TBSP (25 ML) OIL in a large skillet over medium heat until golden. Add salt, turmeric, paprika, cumin, cardamom and pepper flakes and cook for an additional 2 minutes. Add lime juice and crème de banane and slowly stir in cream. Reduce heat to medium-low and simmer until thickened, about 7 to 8 minutes.

Heat remaining oil in a large skillet over medium heat. Add snapper fillets and cook for 2 minutes per side or until lightly browned. Transfer fillets to plates and spoon over sauce. Garnish with cilantro.

Banana Daiquiri

1¾ oz amber rum

½ oz crème de banane

½ oz fresh lime juice

COMBINE RUM, liqueur and lime juice in a cocktail shaker filled with ice and shake vigorously. Strain into a chilled martini glass and garnish with a lime wedge, if desired.

Beeritos

Texturized Vegetable Protein (TVP), which can be found in health or bulk food stores, is a vegetarian staple made from soy flour. It's designed to take on the flavor of whatever it's cooked with and in this recipe those little sponges work their butts off to sop up the beef juices and beer. So, the next time you're chewing on a pepperette outside an abattoir, turn to the protester handcuffed to the door and thank them for TVP.

HEAT OIL IN A LARGE SKILLET over medium-high heat. Add onions, garlic and green pepper and sauté until light brown, about 10 minutes. Remove from heat and set aside.

Brown ground beef in large skillet over medium-high heat. Drain off excess fat. Return to heat, add TVP, ale, tomatoes, salsa, lime juice and sugar and cook for 8 to 10 minutes or until mixture has thickened.

Preheat oven to 350°F (180°C).

Spoon filling onto tortillas, add vegetables and top with cheese. Fold ends over and roll tortillas into burritos, sprinkle with additional cheese and bake for 10 to 12 minutes. Serve with sour cream and chopped green onions.

Classic Margarita

Salt

1½ oz tequila

¾ oz Grand Marnier

½ oz fresh lime juice

RIM MARGARITA GLASS with salt. Combine tequila, Grand Marnier and lime juice in a cocktail shaker filled with ice and shake vigorously. Strain into ice-filled margarita glass and garnish with a lime wedge, if desired.

2 Tbsp (25 mL) vegetable oil

2 large onions, chopped

3 cloves garlic, minced

1 green bell pepper, seeded and chopped

1½ lb (750 g) lean ground beef

¾ cup (175 mL) TVP

1 cup (250 mL) amber ale

3 large tomatoes, chopped

½ cup (125 mL) salsa

1 Tbsp (15 mL) fresh lime juice

2 Tbsp (25 mL) granulated sugar

6 large plain, flour tortillas

2 cups (500 mL) shredded cheddar cheese

¾ cup (175 mL) sour cream

6 green onions, white and green part, chopped

MAKES 6 BURRITOS

Beer Crust Pizza

¾ cup (150 mL) amber ale,
such as Kilkenny

1 tsp (5 mL) granulated sugar

1 tsp (5 mL) active dry yeast

¼ cup (50 mL) extra
virgin olive oil

1 egg at room temperature,
lightly beaten

2 cups (500 mL) all-purpose flour

¼ tsp (1 mL) salt

*Optional: garlic powder, hot
pepper flakes, Italian seasoning,
Parmesan cheese, dried onion,
or dried herbs such as basil,
oregano, etc.*

MAKES ONE 16-INCH
(40-CM) PIZZA
OR TWO 16-INCH (40-CM)
THIN CRUST PIZZAS

Pizza and beer are another of those enduring matches, much like wings and beer, or burgers and beer, or beer and more beer. Adding beer to the dough makes a lighter, flakier crust and gives it a nutty flavor. For a really crisp crust, transfer the rolled-out dough onto a hot pizza stone. The dough can be made up to 3 days in advance and refrigerated. It also freezes for up to 3 months.

HEAT BEER AND SUGAR in a small saucepan over low heat to about 110°F (35°C) (use a candy thermometer). Remove from heat, sprinkle yeast over beer and wait until it dissolves and mixture is foamy, about 10 minutes. Mix in olive oil and egg. Combine dry ingredients in a large bowl and make a well in the center. Add liquid and mix by hand, slowly incorporating flour into the well until dough forms. Turn out onto lightly floured surface and knead for 8 minutes or until dough is smooth and elastic. Place in lightly oiled bowl, cover with plastic wrap and store in warm place for about 2 hours or until dough doubles in size.

Preheat oven to 400°F (200°C).

Punch down dough and roll out onto lightly floured surface. Transfer to pan or hot pizza stone, add toppings and bake for 20 to 25 minutes or until cheese is bubbly and crust is golden.

Boilermaker

1 oz whisky

10 oz lager

POUR WHISKY into a pilsner glass and top with lager.

SUGGESTED PIZZA COMBINATIONS

SANTA FE

Equal parts tomato and barbecue sauce, mozzarella, caramelized onions, cooked chicken, hot peppers and cheddar

MARGUERITE

Tomato sauce, basil, bocconcini, plum tomatoes and fresh black pepper

PARMIGIANO

Pesto, mozzarella, portobello mushrooms, asparagus, Parmesan cheese and bacon

PERUVIAN

Tomato sauce, mozzarella, sundried tomato, basil, red onion, cooked tuna and black olives

TUSCANY

Tomato sauce, mozzarella, portobello mushrooms, sliced Calabrese, black olives and feta

BARBECUE

103

COOKING WITH BOOZE

Lemon-Pepper Souvlaki

½ cup (125 mL)
Limoncello Di Leva

6 boneless, skinless
chicken breasts,
cut into large cubes

¼ cup (50 mL) extra
virgin olive oil

2 cloves garlic, minced

2 Tbsp (25 mL) chopped,
fresh oregano

2 tsp (10 mL) salt

2 tsp (10 mL) freshly
ground black pepper

6 large skewers, soaked
for 30 minutes beforehand

MAKES 6 SERVINGS

Apparently, in medieval times it was standard practice to carry flasks filled with lemon rind and booze. In modern times it's faster to fill your flask with Limoncello Di Leva—and since you've got the bottle open why not make some souvlaki to feed the peasants. The high sugar content caramelizes the chicken, creating a sweet but tart flavor. Just what you need for your next conquest.

COMBINE ⅓ CUP (75 ML) LIMONCELLO DI LEVA, chicken, olive oil, garlic, oregano and salt and pepper in a large bowl, coating chicken thoroughly in marinade. Refrigerate for at least 3 hours or overnight.

Preheat grill to medium-high heat.

Skewer chicken and grill for 15 minutes, rotating as required, until almost fully cooked. Brush with remaining liqueur (stand back!) and cook for additional 2 minutes, or until juices run clear. Serve with lemon wedges, tzatziki and grilled pita.

Iced Limon Tea

1 oz Limoncello Di Leva

4 oz steeped black tea, chilled

Splash cola

COMBINE LIMONCELLO DI LEVA and tea in an old-fashioned glass filled with ice. Top with cola and garnish with a lemon wedge, if desired.

Beer Can Chicken

In this episode our protagonist, Chicken Little, meets a rather unfortunate end, but as recipes go this one's almost impossible to screw up—unless you forget to open the beer. And yes, picking up the chicken by the can and waving it around like you're the Swedish Chef does make it taste better.

PREHEAT GRILL TO HIGH HEAT.

Open beer and drink half.

Take 2 sprigs each of thyme and rosemary and stick them into the beer can. Remove leaves from remaining thyme and rosemary, chop finely and combine with paprika and salt and pepper. Coat chicken in oil and sprinkle with herb mixture. While holding a wing and whispering gently to the wee girl, insert beer can into the chicken's posterior.

Use indirect heat by turning off one side of your grill. Stand chicken on roasting pan on unlit side of grill, close lid and cook for 35 to 45 minutes or until juices run clear and internal temperature reaches 170°F (75°C). Remove from grill and let rest 5 minutes before removing beer can and carving.

Lager and Lime

1 oz lime cordial

16-oz can lager

ADD LIME CORDIAL TO A PILSNER GLASS and top with lager. Garnish with a lime wheel, if desired.

16-oz (500-mL) can
dark or amber beer

6 sprigs fresh thyme

3 sprigs fresh rosemary

1 tsp (5 mL) paprika

1 tsp (5 mL) salt

1 tsp (5 mL) freshly ground
black pepper

3½–5 lb (1.75–2.2 kg) chicken

2 Tbsp (25 mL) extra
virgin olive oil

MAKES 4 SERVINGS

INTO THE FIRE

If you can't use indirect heat or are using a charcoal grill, stand chicken on a foil roasting pan and pour half a can of beer into the bottom to prevent scorching and flare-ups.

Fire-Roasted Mexicano Chicken

¼ cup (50 mL) Kahlúa

¼ cup (50 mL) fresh lime juice

¼ cup (50 mL) extra
virgin olive oil

¼ cup (50 mL) hot sauce

2 cloves garlic

1 onion, quartered

¼ cup (50 mL) cilantro

2 Tbsp (25 mL) fancy molasses

2 Tbsp (25 mL) ketchup

2 tsp (10 mL) Dijon mustard

2 Tbsp (25 mL) pickled jalapeños

1 tsp (5 mL) ground cumin

1 tsp (5 mL) chili powder

1 tsp (5 mL) salt

½ tsp (2 mL) cinnamon

½ tsp (2 mL) nutmeg

¼ tsp (1 mL) freshly
ground black pepper

Pinch hot pepper flakes

4 bone-in chicken breasts,
skin on

MAKES 4 SERVINGS

This jerk-inspired dish combines the unique flavors of Mexico with the fire and spice of a Jamaican barbecue. It's a long shopping list but if you don't have all the spices on hand, get creative and come up with something all your own. We recommend margaritas for inspiration.

COMBINE KAHLÚA, lime juice, olive oil, hot sauce, garlic, onion, cilantro, molasses, ketchup, mustard, jalapeños, cumin, chili powder, salt, cinnamon, nutmeg, black pepper and hot pepper flakes in food processor or blender and blend until smooth. Place chicken breasts in shallow baking dish and pour over marinade. Cover and refrigerate overnight.

Preheat grill to medium-high and sear chicken, breast-side down, for 10 minutes, rotating to produce crisscross grill marks after 5 minutes. Reduce heat to medium, turn chicken, close lid and continue cooking until juices run clear, about 10 minutes.

Raspberry Margaritas

1 cup (250 mL) tequila

1 cup (250 mL) fresh lime juice

¼ cup (50 mL) Chambord

¼ cup (50 mL) sugar

2 cups (500 mL) fresh or frozen raspberries

FILL BLENDER WITH ICE, add tequila, lime juice, Chambord, sugar and raspberries. Blend until smooth. Pour into salt-rimmed glasses and garnish with fresh raspberries and a lime wheel, if desired. MAKES 4 SERVINGS.

BONE OF CONTENTION

Using chicken breasts with the bone-in increases flavor. A whole cut-up chicken, chicken wings or thighs can also be used. Leftover chicken is perfect for soup, sandwiches or a spicy chicken salad.

Mojo Pork Tenderloin

⅓ cup (75 mL) extra
virgin olive oil

6 cloves garlic, minced

1 tsp (5 mL) ground cumin

⅓ cup (75 mL) fresh orange juice

⅓ cup (75 mL) fresh lime juice

⅓ cup (75 mL) dark rum

1 Tbsp (15 mL) grated
orange zest

¼ tsp (1 mL)
dried oregano

Salt

Freshly ground
black pepper

2 pork tenderloins
(¾ lb/375 g each)

3 Tbsp (45 mL)
chopped cilantro

MAKES 6 SERVINGS

COOKING WITH BOOZE

ZEN AND THE ART OF MUDDLING

Muddling citrus fruits and herbs releases natural oils packed with flavor. The technique takes a bit of practice but the results are well worth it. The sugar provides friction, aiding in the process. Over-muddling will result in pulverized mint, which may get stuck in your guests' teeth. Under-muddling will prevent the oils from being released and the flavors won't integrate. Place ingredients in an old-fashioned glass or small pitcher if making for a crowd. Use a wooden muddler or the end of a wooden spoon and squeeze ingredients against the sides and bottom of the glass until fragrant.

Leaving aside Fidel, cigars and, perhaps, a small issue with missiles, Cuba is best known for its mojitos and mojo. Mojo, Cuba's national sauce, serves many purposes—a marinade, serving sauce and even a sandwich spread. The warm sweetness of the rum, mixed with cumin and toasted garlic, is perfectly suited for pork. Americans in particular will appreciate this communist treat, served with Cohiba cigars and cold mojitos.

HEAT OIL IN SKILLET over medium heat and add garlic and cumin, stirring for 2 to 3 minutes or until golden. Add juices, rum, zest, oregano and salt and pepper to taste and bring to a boil. Cook for 3 minutes, remove from heat, transfer to bowl and refrigerate until cool. Place pork in shallow dish and pour over marinade. Refrigerate for 1 to 3 hours.

Grease and preheat grill to medium heat.

Grill tenderloin for 25 minutes, turning twice, or until internal temperature reaches 150°F (65°C), for medium. Transfer to cutting board and tent with aluminum foil.

Meanwhile, bring marinade to boil in small saucepan over medium-high heat and cook for 3 to 4 minutes, or until reduced and slightly thickened. Remove from heat and add cilantro. Slice pork into medallions and arrange on serving platter. Spoon over sauce and garnish with orange slices, if desired.

Mojito

½ lime, cut into quarters

3 sprigs fresh mint

1 tsp (5 mL) granulated sugar

1½ oz amber rum

Soda

SQUEEZE JUICE from lime quarters into an old-fashioned glass. Toss in lime quarters, sugar and mint and muddle with the end of a wooden spoon until sugar is dissolved. Add ice and rum and top with soda. Garnish with a sprig of mint and a lime wheel, if desired.

Caribbean Pork *with* Corn and Papaya Salsa

The spices of the Caribbean islands inspire this fragrant pork tenderloin. When topped with corn salsa this dish becomes the perfect marriage between crisp and meaty textures and spicy-sweet flavors. If you don't have Xanté you can substitute another cognac but it's surprising how much flavor a little Xanté can add to this dish.

REMOVE ANY EXCESS FAT from tenderloins and brush with olive oil. Combine brown sugar, allspice, cardamom, cumin and turmeric in a small bowl and drizzle with cognac. Rub mixture evenly over pork, cover and refrigerate for 3 hours or overnight.

Meanwhile, combine corn, papaya, onion, cilantro, jalapeño, lime juice and salt and pepper. Cover and refrigerate until ready to use. This will keep in refrigerator for up to 2 days.

Preheat grill to high.

Grill tenderloins for 5 to 6 minutes per side or until internal temperature reaches 150°F (65°C), for medium. Remove from grill, tent with aluminum foil and let rest for 5 minutes. Slice pork into medallions and serve with salsa.

Xanté Lemonade

¾ oz Xanté Poire au Cognac

½ oz Absolut Kurant vodka

8 oz pink lemonade

COMBINE COGNAC, vodka and lemonade in a Collins glass filled with ice and garnish with a lemon wheel, if desired.

PORK

2 pork tenderloins
(¾ lb/375 g each)

1 Tbsp (15 mL) extra virgin olive oil

1 Tbsp (15 mL) packed brown sugar

1 tsp (5 mL) allspice

1 tsp (5 mL) ground cardamom

1 tsp (5 mL) ground cumin

1 tsp (5 mL) turmeric

1 tsp (5 mL) Xanté Poire au Cognac

CORN AND PAPAYA SALSA

1 cup (250 mL) corn
(fresh or frozen)

1 cup (250 mL) diced papaya

¾ cup (175 mL)
red onion, chopped

½ cup (125 mL)
chopped cilantro

1 jalapeño pepper,
seeded and minced

1 Tbsp (15 mL) fresh lime juice

½ tsp (2 mL) salt

Freshly ground black pepper

MAKES 6 SERVINGS

Cuba Libre Back Ribs

Larry Jennings, the BB gun-wielding patriarch of Ryan's family, has two decrees: "Never do anything half-assed" and "Nobody makes ribs like I do." We took up his challenge and we're pretty sure this recipe qualifies as whole-assed. You be the judge.

PREHEAT OVEN TO 200°F (95°C).

For the ribs, trim any visible fat and remove membrane from underside if attached. Season both sides with salt and pepper and place meat-side down in large baking dish. Arrange onion and garlic evenly around ribs. Pour enough cola to cover ribs completely. Cover with aluminum foil and bake for 3 hours. Remove from oven and allow ribs to come to room temperature in cooking liquid, about 1½ hours.

Meanwhile, to make the sauce, heat oil in small saucepan over medium heat. Add onion, garlic, cumin and chili powder and cook for 5 minutes, stirring constantly. Add ketchup, rum, brown sugar, vinegar, mustard, Worcestershire sauce and hot pepper sauce and simmer for 15 minutes.

Preheat grill to low.

Place ribs meat-side down on grill and close lid. Cook, turning occasionally, until meat is browned and caramelized, about 30 to 45 minutes, or until tender and bones are exposed at ends. With 10 minutes remaining, brush ribs with barbecue sauce. Cut into 3-rib pieces and serve.

Cuba Libre

This drink literally means "free Cuba" but really it's just fancy bartender talk for a classic rum and Coke.

1½ oz white rum

4 oz Coca-Cola

Splash of fresh lime juice

COMBINE RUM, Coca-Cola and lime juice in an old-fashioned glass filled with ice and garnish with a lime wedge, if desired.

RIBS

2 racks pork back ribs

1 tsp (5 mL) salt

½ tsp (2 mL) freshly ground black pepper

1 onion, peeled and quartered

6 cloves garlic, crushed

8 cups (2 L) cola

CARIBBEAN BARBECUE SAUCE

1 tsp (5 mL) vegetable oil

1 onion, minced

1 clove garlic, minced

1 tsp (5 mL) ground cumin

1 tsp (5 mL) chili powder

¾ cup (175 mL) ketchup

⅓ cup (75 mL) dark rum

¼ cup (50 mL) packed brown sugar

¼ cup (50 mL) cider vinegar

1 Tbsp (15 mL) Dijon mustard

1 Tbsp (15 mL) Worcestershire sauce

Dash hot pepper sauce

MAKES 4 SERVINGS

Mustard-Glazed Brats *with* Caramelized Onions

CARAMELIZED ONIONS

2 Tbsp (25 mL) butter

1 Vidalia onion, sliced

¼ cup (50 mL) sweet sherry

Pinch salt

MUSTARD GLAZE

½ cup (125 mL) Dijon mustard

¼ cup (50 mL) packed
brown sugar

2 Tbsp (25 mL) fancy molasses

1 clove garlic, minced

¼ cup (50 mL) bourbon

¼ cup (50 mL)
fresh orange juice

Dash hot pepper sauce

6 bratwurst sausages

6 sausage buns

MAKES 6 SERVINGS

In a city like Toronto, where hotdog vendors pop up like Starbucks, you learn a few things pretty quickly: 1. mayonnaise is not an August condiment; 2. cheese is only legal in alternating years; 3. you can always do better at home.

FOR THE ONIONS, melt butter in medium non-stick skillet over medium heat. Add onion and cook until translucent, about 10 minutes. Reduce heat to medium-low, add sherry and salt and cook until very soft and golden brown, about 20 minutes. Set aside.

Meanwhile, to make the glaze, whisk together mustard, brown sugar, molasses and garlic in a small saucepan. Add bourbon, orange juice and hot pepper sauce and whisk until combined. Bring to a boil over medium heat. Reduce heat to low and simmer for 20 to 25 minutes or until glaze thickens slightly.

Preheat grill to medium.

Grill sausages for 15 to 20 minutes, turning occasionally until cooked. Reduce heat to low, brush sausages with glaze and cook for an additional 5 minutes, brushing with more glaze as required. Serve with toasted buns and caramelized onions.

Mint Julep

4 sprigs fresh mint

1 tsp (5 mL) granulated sugar

2 tsp (10 mL) water

2½ oz bourbon

MUDDLE MINT LEAVES with sugar and water in a Collins glass. Fill with crushed ice and top with bourbon. Garnish with another mint sprig, if desired.

Asian Barbecued Sirloin

½ cup (125 mL) light soy sauce

¼ cup (50 mL) pure
maple syrup (see page 18)

2 cloves garlic, minced

1 Tbsp (15 mL) grated fresh ginger

1 tsp (5 mL) Dijon mustard

½ tsp (2 mL) sesame oil

½ tsp (2 mL) hot pepper flakes

½ cup (125 mL) amber ale

2 lb (1 kg) sirloin steak

1 Tbsp (15 mL) butter

MAKES 4 SERVINGS

This marinade is deep and slightly sweet. The beer prevents it from overpowering the natural flavor of our favorite bovine-based product and it works equally well with chicken, pork or kebabs. We show you road, you find way, grasshopper.

COMBINE SOY SAUCE, maple syrup, garlic, ginger, mustard, oil and pepper flakes in medium bowl. Slowly add beer and mix well. Consume any remaining beer immediately.

Place steak in ceramic or glass baking dish and cover with marinade. Cover and marinate at room temperature for 1 hour.

Lightly grease grill and preheat to high.

Place steak on grill and cook for about 5 minutes. Turn, splash on a little more marinade and cook for an additional 5 minutes for medium-rare, depending on thickness. Remove from grill, top with butter and allow to rest for 3 to 4 minutes. Slice against the grain into ½-inch (1-cm) strips and transfer to serving platter.

Soho Coladas

¾ cup (175 mL) crème de banane

⅓ cup (75 mL) coconut rum

2 Tbsp (25 mL) Soho lychee liqueur

1 banana

2 cups (500 mL) milk

COMBINE CRÈME DE BANANE, rum, Soho liqueur, banana and milk in blender filled with ice and blend until smooth. Pour into sugar-rimmed margarita glasses and garnish with a piece of pineapple, if desired. MAKES 4 SERVINGS.

Royal Beefeater Burgers *with* Cognac Ketchup

BURGERS

3 lb (1.5 kg) medium ground beef

1 onion, minced

2 cloves garlic, minced

½ cup (125 mL) breadcrumbs

2 eggs

3 Tbsp (45 mL) gin

2 tsp (10 mL) sesame oil

2 tsp (10 mL) salt

2 tsp (10 mL) freshly ground black pepper

COGNAC KETCHUP

½ cup (125 mL) ketchup

½ cup (125 mL) chili sauce

¼ cup (50 mL) cognac

2 Tbsp (25 mL) butter

1 Tbsp (15 mL) balsamic vinegar

¼ tsp (1 mL) ground cumin

Pinch cayenne

¼ tsp (1 mL) allspice

Dash hot pepper sauce

MAKES 8 PATTIES AND
1 ¼ CUPS (300 ML)
OF KETCHUP

Burgers are back in vogue as part of the comfort food movement, and some of the best restaurants are now serving them to the high-market crowd at high-market prices. Slap these beauties on fancy bread like focaccia, add a sprig of rosemary and sell them to your friends for 35 bucks a bun.

COMBINE BEEF, onion, garlic and breadcrumbs in large bowl. In a separate bowl lightly whisk eggs with gin, sesame oil and salt and pepper. Fold egg mixture into beef and mix until just combined—overmixing will produce tough patties. Divide mixture into 8 patties.

Preheat grill to high.

Place burgers over flame and cook for 6 to 8 minutes per side or until juices run clear. Serve on toasted buns with cognac ketchup and your favorite toppings.

To make the ketchup, combine ketchup, chili sauce, cognac, butter, vinegar, cumin, cayenne, allspice and pepper sauce in a small saucepan over low heat and simmer for about 15 minutes, stirring regularly. Refrigerate until cool before serving. Ketchup will keep in the refrigerator for up to a month.

Bronx

2 oz gin

1 oz orange juice

½ oz sweet vermouth

½ oz dry vermouth

COMBINE GIN, orange juice, sweet vermouth and dry vermouth in a cocktail shaker filled with ice and shake vigorously. Strain into a chilled martini glass and garnish with an orange slice, if desired.

Thai Shrimp and Mango Kabobs

These sweet and spicy kabobs are easy to prepare and are perfect for summer entertaining on the patio. As an added bonus, after a few glasses of sangria you'll discover skewers are great for hand-to-hand combat—place corks on tips to prevent injury.

SOAK SKEWERS IN WARM WATER for 30 minutes to prevent scorching on the grill.

Heat water, vinegar and sugar in small saucepan over medium heat until sugar dissolves. Remove from heat and let cool. Add liqueur, lime juice, garlic and pepper flakes.

Assemble 3 shrimp and 4 mango pieces on each skewer, alternating between fruit and shrimp. Arrange in a single layer in a baking dish and pour over marinade. Refrigerate for 30 minutes, turning once.

Preheat grill to medium-high.

Place kabobs on grill, close lid and cook for 3 minutes per side or until shrimp are bright pink and firm. Be careful not to overcook.

4 large bamboo skewers

¼ cup (50 mL) water

¼ cup (50 mL) rice vinegar

2 Tbsp (25 mL) granulated sugar

¼ cup (50 mL) Alizé Gold Passion liqueur

2 Tbsp (25 mL) fresh lime juice

1 garlic clove, minced

½ tsp (2 mL) hot pepper flakes

12 jumbo shrimp (11 to 15 count), deveined and peeled

2 semi-ripe mangos, peeled and each cut into 8 bite-size pieces

MAKES 4 SERVINGS

Peach and White Wine Sangria

1 bottle (750 mL) sweet Riesling

½ cup (125 mL) Alizé Gold Passion liqueur

½ cup (125 mL) peach purée or peach juice

¼ cup (50 mL) granulated sugar

Slices of peach, apple and assorted citrus fruits

Soda

COMBINE WINE, Alizé, peach purée, sugar and fruit in large pitcher and refrigerate for at least 3 hours or overnight. Fill wineglasses three-quarters full and top with soda. Garnish with frozen cranberries, if desired.
MAKES 4 GENEROUS SERVINGS.

Tequila Mockingbird Fajitas

1–1½ lb (500–750 g)
beef flank steak

¼ cup (50 mL) tequila

¼ cup (50 mL) extra
virgin olive oil

2 Tbsp (25 mL) ketchup

2 Tbsp (25 mL) fresh lime juice

1 clove garlic, minced

1 Tbsp (15 mL) chili powder

1 Tbsp (15 mL) cocoa powder

½ tsp (2 mL) cayenne pepper

2 tsp (10 mL) salt

½ tsp (2 mL) freshly
ground black pepper

1 red bell pepper, sliced

1 green bell pepper, sliced

1 red onion, sliced

1½ cups (375 mL)
sliced mushrooms

8 medium flour tortillas

2 cups (500 mL) shredded
Monterey Jack

Chopped fresh tomatoes

Chopped fresh cilantro

Guacamole

Sour cream

MAKES 4 SERVINGS

It's difficult to believe that a troublemaker like tequila is made from a member of the lily family—the blue agave plant. Then again, tequila's not the first time evil spawn came from fair stock: Ryan's parents are lovely people. We classify tequila, like gin, as an "opinionated" drink, so have your friends over for these fajitas, a few tequila sunrises and steer the conversation toward religion and politics.

TRIM FLANK STEAK of any excess fat and place in shallow baking dish. Whisk tequila, 2 Tbsp (25 mL) olive oil, ketchup, lime juice, garlic, chili powder, cocoa, cayenne, and salt and pepper together in a medium-sized bowl. Pour marinade over steak and refrigerate for at least 6 hours or overnight.

Preheat grill to high.

Grill steak until desired doneness is reached, about 3 minutes per side for medium-rare. Allow beef to rest for 3 to 4 minutes in a covered dish then cut against the grain into ½-inch (1-cm) slices.

Meanwhile, heat remaining olive oil in a large skillet over high heat and sauté bell peppers, onion and mushrooms until softened.

Serve beef and sautéed vegetables on warmed tortillas, topped with shredded cheese. Garnish with fresh tomatoes, cilantro, guacamole and sour cream.

Tequila Sunrise

¾ oz grenadine

2 oz tequila

8 oz orange juice

POUR GRENADINE into a collins glass. Add ice, tequila and orange juice. Serve with a straw and garnish with an orange wheel, if desired.

DESSERTS

COOKING WITH BOOZE

Mohawk Peaches

½ cup (125 mL) butter

2 Tbsp (25 mL) packed
brown sugar

½ cup (125 mL) amber rum

10 peaches, peeled and sliced

6 Belgian waffles,
cut in half diagonally

4 cups (1 L) vanilla ice cream

1 cup (250 mL) fresh
wild blueberries

MAKES 6 SERVINGS

You'll want to get to know these peaches. They're sweet and charming and punked-out with just enough sass to make you want to lock up your daughters. To save time, make the waffles ahead or buy them fresh from the bread aisle—we won't tell.

HEAT BUTTER in a large non-stick skillet over medium-high heat until foaming. Add sugar and cook, stirring until dissolved. Add rum and cook for 5 minutes, or until sauce is slightly reduced. Add peaches and cook 2 minutes until slightly softened but still firm. Remove from heat.

Arrange waffle halves on plate so one is lying down and the other is standing vertically beside it. Place a large scoop of ice cream onto plate and spoon over peaches. Top with a spoonful of blueberries.

Blueberry Tea

1 oz amaretto

1 oz Grand Marnier

Steeped Earl Grey tea

COMBINE AMARETTO and Grand Marnier in a specialty coffee glass and top with hot tea. Garnish with an orange twist, if desired.

Grapefruit and Gin Granita

1 cup (250 mL) granulated sugar

2 red grapefruit,
segmented and seeded

1 cup (250 mL)
ruby grapefruit juice

1½ Tbsp (20 mL) gin

MAKES 6 SERVINGS

Grapefruit and gin go together like rock stars and bad habits. Grapefruit brings out the whole spice rack of flavorings that are used to make gin, including lemon, orange, cardamom, coriander, orris root, angelica root and, of course, juniper berries. The combination of the sweet, tart grapefruit mixed with the dry floral notes of the gin make this adult-oriented slush a refreshing summer dessert to enjoy late into the evening. Send the kids to bed early, dip into the freezer and start your own bad habit.

COMBINE 1 CUP (250 ML) OF WATER with ¾ cup (175 mL) sugar in a small saucepan and bring to a boil. Remove from heat, allow to cool, then pour over grapefruit segments and refrigerate until ready to use.

Combine ½ cup (125 mL) water and remaining sugar in a medium saucepan and bring to a boil. Add grapefruit juice and gin and pour into shallow baking dish and freeze for about an hour. To ensure even consistency mix granita every 20 minutes with fork, working from outer edges in.

Place a few grapefruit segments into martini glasses and top with 1 scoop of granita. Drizzle a spoonful of sugar syrup over each glass and serve.

Pink Tart

1½ oz gin

4 oz lemonade

4 oz raspberry juice

COMBINE GIN, lemonade and raspberry juice in a Collins glass filled with ice and garnish with a few fresh raspberries, if desired.

GRAND OLD LADY

The Black Friars distillery in Plymouth, England, is home to Plymouth Gin. It is the oldest working gin distillery, with records going back to 1697. By 1850 Plymouth gin had gained worldwide exposure as the "Gin of the Royal Navy" and, in 1896, the first recorded recipe for a Dry Martini specified Plymouth gin as an ingredient (as printed in *Stuart's Fancy Drinks and How to Mix Them*). By the 1930s Plymouth was the star of the cocktail era.

Summer Berry Icewine Sabayon

1 cup (250 mL) fresh strawberries, quartered

1 cup (250 mL) fresh raspberries

1 cup (250 mL) fresh blackberries

1 cup (250 mL) fresh blueberries

½ cup (125 mL) granulated sugar

5 egg yolks

¼ cup (50 mL) icewine

MAKES 4–6 SERVINGS

This light summer dessert is a refreshing treat when the mercury climbs. A sabayon is a foamy mixture of eggs, sugar and liquor, in this case icewine. Sherry, light fruit liqueurs and late harvest Riesling also work especially well.

PLACE MARTINI GLASSES in the freezer to chill.

Combine fruit with ¼ cup (50 mL) of the sugar, cover and refrigerate until ready to use.

Whisk remaining sugar, egg yolks and icewine in a metal bowl over a *bain-marie* (pot of gently simmering water) until thick and foamy, about 5 minutes. (Mixture should triple in size.) Adjust heat so mixture never gets too hot, or eggs may scramble. Spoon berries into chilled martini glasses, top with sabayon and serve.

To serve your sabayon chilled, remove from stove and whisk until cool. Refrigerate until cold and then spoon over berries.

Cool Blue

1½ oz vodka

1 oz Hpnotiq liqueur

½ oz fresh lemon juice

COMBINE VODKA, Hpnotiq and lemon juice in a cocktail shaker filled with ice and strain into a chilled martini glass. Garnish with a lemon twist, if desired.

ICEWINE 101

Icewine, originally *eiswein*, was reputedly invented by accident in Germany in the 1700s. It's a rare form of wine produced from grapes that have been naturally frozen on the vine. The grapes are then harvested and pressed while still frozen. This process traps the water crystals in the grape during the pressing and the grape releases only 5% to 10% of its normal juice quantity. This coveted liquid is defined by its intense flavor and richness in sugar.

Passion Fruit Crème Brûlée

8 egg yolks

½ cup (125 mL) granulated sugar

2 cups (500 mL) heavy cream (38%)

1 tsp (5 mL) vanilla

¼ cup (50 mL) Alizé Red Passion liqueur

MAKES 4 SERVINGS

Finally, a recipe that combines alcohol and a blowtorch! If you don't already own a torch this is the perfect opportunity to put on the biggest belt buckle you have and head to the hardware store. You can also use a small kitchen torch to caramelize the sugar. (But what will you use to fix your pipes?)

PREHEAT OVEN TO 300°F (150°C).

Whisk together egg yolks and ⅓ cup (75 mL) sugar in a large bowl until sugar dissolves and eggs are light and fluffy. Whisk in cream and vanilla. Divide mixture among 4 ramekins and place into a 9- × 13-inch (23- × 33-cm) baking dish. Fill the dish with water three-quarters of the way up the ramekins.

Bake until cups are set around the edges but still wobbly in the center, about 60 to 70 minutes. Remove cups from oven and water bath and allow to cool on rack. Refrigerate for 2 hours or overnight.

When ready to serve, sprinkle about ½ tsp (2 mL) sugar over each ramekin. Caramelize the sugar by passing the torch over the top of the ramekin in an even motion until sugar melts and bubbles. Be careful not to scorch. Allow to stand for a couple of minutes before serving.

Alizé Royale

1 oz Alizé Red Passion liqueur

5 oz champagne

ADD ALIZÉ TO FLUTE and top with champagne.

HOT TOPIC

Some recipes claim that you can caramelize the sugar under your broiler. We've never had any success with this method—the heat re-cooks the custard and curdles it. Go buy a blowtorch already!

White Chocolate and Raspberry Panna Cotta

1 cup (250 mL) heavy cream (38%)

¼ cup (50 mL) white crème de cacao

¾ cup + 1 Tbsp (190 mL) granulated sugar

1 package unflavored gelatin (2¼ tsp/11 mL)

¾ cup (175 mL) milk

1½ cups (375 mL) fresh raspberries

2 Tbsp (25 mL) triple sec

1 tsp (5 mL) fresh lemon juice

MAKES 4 SERVINGS

This smooth and decedent dessert is Italy's answer to crème brûlée. Panna cotta translates to "cooked cream" and uses gelatin instead of egg yolks as a thickening agent, making it lighter than crème brûlée but with almost the same consistency. We suggest going all the way and making this white chocolate wonder with its little red raspberry bobbles, but feel free to break open that liquor cabinet and get inventive—orange, lychee, mint, butterscotch, etc.

COMBINE CREAM, crème de cacao and ⅓ cup (75 mL) sugar in a medium saucepan over medium heat, stirring constantly until sugar dissolves and mixture becomes slightly frothy around edges. Remove from heat and set aside.

Sprinkle gelatin over milk in small saucepan and set over low heat until dissolved. Stir into cream mixture. Pour into 4 ramekins and refrigerate for 4 hours or until set.

Meanwhile, combine 1¼ cups (325 mL) of the raspberries with remaining sugar, triple sec and lemon juice in a saucepan over medium heat. Stir until sugar dissolves and raspberries are soft. Remove from heat and pour raspberries through a fine sieve to remove seeds. Stir in remaining raspberries and refrigerate until ready to serve.

Place ramekins in hot water bath for about 10 seconds to loosen panna cotta and invert onto plates. Spoon over raspberries and serve.

White Chocolate Raspberry Martini

2 oz raspberry vodka

1 oz white crème de cacao

COMBINE VODKA and crème de cacao in a cocktail shaker filled with ice and shake vigorously. Strain into a chilled martini glass and garnish with a sprig of mint, if desired.

Individual Tia Maria Semifreddos

Semifreddo, Italian for half-frozen, is the ultimate summer dessert. Much easier to make than ice cream, semifreddos don't require special machines or brine mixtures and have a light, ultra-smooth texture. If you happened to finish off your last bottle of Tia Maria over a heated game of Boggle, try Bailey's, Grand Marnier, Amarula or another favorite liqueur instead.

WHISK EGGS AND YOLKS, sugar and Tia Maria in a large metal bowl over a *bain-marie* (pot of gently simmering water) until sugar dissolves and mixture is thick and frothy, about 4 to 5 minutes. Remove from heat, add cream of tartar, and beat with an electric mixer until thick. Set aside. Whip cream with an electric mixer in a large bowl until soft peaks form. Gently fold egg mixture into whipped cream. Pour into small cocktail glasses, cover with aluminum foil and freeze for 2 hours.

Scoop out the center of the semifreddo with a melon baller warmed under hot water and pour in the liqueur of your choice.

Creamy Dream

1½ oz Amarula

½ oz butterscotch liqueur

6 oz milk

COMBINE AMARULA, butterscotch liqueur and milk in a cocktail shaker filled with ice and strain into a Collins glass filled with ice. Garnish with an espresso bean, if desired.

4 large eggs plus 2 yolks, at room temperature

1 cup (250 mL) super-fine sugar

¼ cup (50 mL) Tia Maria

½ tsp (2 mL) cream of tartar

1¾ cups (425 mL) cold heavy cream (38%)

MAKES 6 SERVINGS

Apple Beignets *with* Calvados Cream

APPLE BEIGNETS

1 cup (250 mL) all-purpose flour

¼ tsp (1 mL) salt

1 Tbsp (15 mL) instant yeast

½ cup (125 mL) warm flat lager

¼ cup (50 mL) warm apple juice

1 Tbsp (15 mL) butter, melted

¼ cup (50 mL) Calvados

2 Tbsp (25 mL) confectioner's sugar, plus extra for dusting beignets

4 Royal Gala apples, each peeled and sliced into 8 segments

1 egg white

12 cups (3 L) vegetable oil, for frying

CALVADOS CREAM

1 cup (250 mL) heavy cream (38%)

2 Tbsp (25 mL) Calvados

2 tsp (10 mL) confectioner's sugar

MAKES 12 BEIGNETS

If you have a hole in the middle, you're a doughnut. If you're poured into the deep-fryer, you're a funnel cake, but if you're covered in confectioner's sugar and living in New Orleans, you're a beignet (pronounced ben-yay*). Brought over from France and popularized by legendary New Orleans eatery Café Du Monde, the beignet was originally a savory dinner item but was adapted to satisfy the demand for morning pastries.*

TO MAKE THE BEIGNETS, sift flour and salt into a large bowl. Form a well in the center. Put yeast, beer, apple juice and melted butter into the well. Slowly mix the batter together, working small amounts of dry ingredients into the well until all ingredients are mixed and batter is smooth. Cover bowl with plastic wrap and place in warm location for about 3 hours, or until doubled in size.

Meanwhile, mix Calvados and sugar in medium bowl and soak apple segments, allowing them to macerate until batter is ready.

Preheat oil in large pot or Dutch oven to 350°F (180°C) on kitchen thermometer.

Stiffly beat egg white and fold into batter. Use a slotted or wire mesh spoon to dip apple segments into batter and slowly lower into hot oil. Deep-fry beignets in batches until golden brown, turning once, about 3 minutes. Remove from oil and allow to cool on wire rack placed over newspaper.

Whip heavy cream, Calvados and sugar together until stiff peaks form.

Dust beignets with confectioner's sugar and serve warm with Calvados cream.

Apple Martini

1 oz vanilla vodka

1 oz vodka

1 oz Calvados

Dash Cointreau

COMBINE VODKAS, Calvados and Cointreau in a cocktail shaker filled with ice and shake vigorously. Strain into a chilled martini glass and garnish with an apple slice, if desired.

Caramel Apple Fondue

This recipe conjures up memories of country fairs and sweet fall flavors and will have you scraping the bottom of the fondue pot for every last drop of caramel. We were scraping the bottom of the barrel when we came up with this recipe! Kidding, kidding.

DISSOLVE SUGAR in ¼ cup (50 mL) water in a medium saucepan over low heat. Increase heat to medium, bring to a boil and cook without stirring until a deep caramel color is reached, about 3 to 4 minutes. If sugar crystals cling to the edge of the pan, brush sides with a wet pastry brush. Whisk in cream a little at a time until sauce is smooth, about 5 minutes. Add Calvados and cook 1 minute longer. Remove from heat, add butter and stir until butter melts.

Transfer to a fondue pot and serve with fresh fruit and cookies.

Caramel Apple Martini

1 oz apple vodka

1 oz sour apple liqueur

1 oz butterscotch liqueur

COMBINE APPLE VODKA, sour apple and butterscotch ripple liqueur in a cocktail shaker filled with ice and shake vigorously. Strain into a chilled martini glass and garnish with an apple slice.

1 cup (250 mL) granulated sugar

2½ cups (625 mL) heavy cream (38%), at room temperature

¼ cup (50 mL) Calvados

2 Tbsp (25 mL) unsalted butter

Sliced green apples, pears, strawberries, etc.

Shortbread cookies

MAKES 6 SERVINGS

DESSERTS

CANDY LAND

Caramel can be prepared ahead of time and reheated over low heat just before serving.

B-52 Cupcakes

CUPCAKES

2 cups (500 mL) all-purpose flour

1 cup (250 mL) granulated sugar

¼ cup (50 mL) cocoa

1½ tsp (7 mL) baking soda

1 tsp (5 mL) baking powder

1 cup (250 mL) mayonnaise
(full-fat is best)

½ cup (125 mL) brewed espresso
or strong coffee, cooled

¼ cup (50 mL) Kahlúa

1½ cups (375 mL) heavy
cream (38%)

¼ cup (50 mL) Bailey's
Irish Cream

¼ cup (50 mL)
confectioner's sugar

1 tsp (5 mL) unflavored gelatin

CANDIED ORANGE ZEST

1 medium orange

½ cup (125 mL) granulated sugar

2 Tbsp (25 mL) Grand Marnier

MAKES 48 MINI OR
12 REGULAR CUPCAKES

COOKING WITH BOOZE

Inspired by the sweet and creamy shooter, with a gentle nod to the group that brought us "Rock Lobster," these little beauties are an instant party hit. With full bottles of Kahlúa, Bailey's and Grand Marnier on hand, baking these is almost as much fun as eating them.

PREHEAT OVEN TO 350°F (180°C). Line muffin tins with paper baking cups.

Mix flour, sugar, cocoa, baking soda and baking powder in large bowl and form a well in the center. Add mayonnaise, ½ cup (125 mL) water, espresso, and 2 tsp (10 mL) Kahlúa and mix with wooden spoon until smooth. Fill cups two-thirds full with batter and bake until toothpick inserted in center comes out clean (15 minutes for mini or 25 minutes for regular muffins). Remove from oven and let stand for 5 minutes, remove from pan and allow to cool completely on rack. Brush remaining Kahlúa over cupcakes.

Meanwhile, combine heavy cream, Bailey's and sugar in medium bowl and beat with electric mixer until stiff peaks form. Sprinkle gelatin over 2 Tbsp (25 mL) of water in small saucepan and place over low heat until gelatin dissolves. Remove from heat and let cool slightly. Drizzle gelatin into cream mixture and beat on low speed until combined.

Fit pastry bag with round tip and fill with whipped cream. Pipe swirls of cream onto each cupcake and garnish with candied orange zest or pieces of grated fresh zest.

To make the zest, peel orange very thinly with vegetable peeler, making sure to get only zest and no bitter pith. Slice into thin strips. Place zest in small saucepan and cover with cold water. Place over medium-high heat and boil until zest is slightly translucent, about 15 minutes. Add sugar, Grand Marnier and ½ cup (125 mL) water. Bring to a boil, lower heat and simmer until zest becomes completely translucent, about 1 hour. Remove zest from syrup, separate strands and place on wax paper to cool.

Love Shake

1 oz Kahlúa

1½ oz Bailey's Irish Cream

Splash Grand Marnier

1 oz brewed espresso

4 oz milk

COMBINE KAHLÚA, Bailey's, Grand Marnier, espresso and milk in a cocktail shaker filled with ice and shake vigorously. Strain into a pilsner glass and serve with a straw.

IN THE BAG

To save time and mess use a pastry bag to pipe batter into the paper baking cups.

Coconut Cake *with* Godiva Buttercream

CAKE

1¾ cups (425 mL) cake-and-pastry flour, sifted

2¼ tsp (11 mL) baking powder

¾ tsp (4 mL) salt

½ cup (125 mL) butter, softened

1 cup + 2 Tbsp (280 mL) granulated sugar

2 eggs

⅔ cup (150 mL) coconut milk

1 tsp (5 mL) vanilla

⅔ cup (150 mL) sweetened flaked coconut

GODIVA BUTTERCREAM

5 large egg whites

½ tsp (2 mL) cream of tartar

1 cup (250 mL) granulated sugar

¼ cup (50 mL) water

2 cups (500 mL) cold unsalted butter, cut into small cubes

⅓ cup (75 mL) Godiva White Chocolate Cream liqueur

¾ cup (175 mL) sweetened flaked coconut (to garnish)

MAKES 10 SERVINGS

We knew the title would get your attention. Can't you just imagine staring at her beautiful milky white curves as your tongue gently caresses her sweet coconut, penetrating her silken white chocolate and transforming it into a velvet cream? She teases you to take a bite, but you resist, treasuring the moment. Filled with anticipation, you can hold on no longer and plunge deep into her fluffy center, again and again, until the two of you become one entity, breathing hard and satiated. Or maybe that's just us.

PREHEAT OVEN TO 350°F (180°C). Grease and flour two 8-inch (20-cm) round cake pans and line bottoms with parchment paper.

Combine flour, baking powder and salt in a medium bowl and set aside. Cream butter and sugar together with electric mixer until light and fluffy, about 5 minutes. Add eggs, one at a time, beating well after each addition.

Add half of the flour mixture and half of the coconut milk, then repeat, beating after each addition until smooth. Stir in vanilla and coconut.

Pour batter into prepared pans and bake for 30 to 35 minutes or until toothpick inserted in center comes out clean. Remove from oven and cool in pans for 10 minutes, then invert onto racks and cool completely before frosting.

BUTTER'S BETTER

Store buttercream at room temperature for 2 days or refrigerate for up to 10 days. Allow buttercream to come to room temperature and beat before using.

To make the buttercream, beat egg whites with an electric mixer until soft peaks form. Add cream of tartar and continue beating until stiff peaks form. Meanwhile, combine sugar and water in a small non-stick saucepan over medium-high heat, stirring constantly until sugar dissolves. Bring mixture to a boil, stop stirring and boil syrup until it reaches 248°F (120°C) on a candy thermometer. Slowly pour syrup into egg whites while beating on high speed, being careful not to let syrup hit beaters, spinning it onto the sides of the bowl. Once all syrup is combined reduce speed to medium and continue beating until smooth. Add butter, a piece at a time, until completely incorporated and buttercream is smooth. Lower speed and drizzle in liqueur. Cool at room temperature before assembling cake.

To assemble cake, spread one-third of frosting over first layer. Top with second layer and remaining frosting. Garnish with flaked coconut.

Coco Loco

1½ oz coconut rum

1½ oz Godiva White Chocolate Cream liqueur

2 oz milk

COMBINE RUM, liqueur and milk in a cocktail shaker filled with ice and shake vigorously. Strain into a chilled martini glass and dust with cinnamon, if desired.

Goldschläger and Dark Chocolate Layer Cake

CAKE

2 cups (500 mL) cake-and-pastry
flour, sifted

1 cup (250 mL) granulated sugar

2 Tbsp (25 mL) cocoa

1 tsp (5 mL) baking powder

1½ tsp (7 mL) baking soda

1 cup (250 mL) mayonnaise

¾ cup (175 mL) cold water

¼ cup (50 mL) Goldschläger

GOLDSCHLÄGER BUTTERCREAM

4 egg yolks

½ cup + 2 Tbsp (150 mL)
granulated sugar

2 oz (50 g) bittersweet chocolate,
chopped

¼ cup (50 mL) water

1 cup (250 mL) unsalted butter,
cut into small cubes

2 Tbsp (25 mL) Goldschläger

DARK CHOCOLATE GANACHE

1 cup (250 mL) heavy cream
(38%)

8 oz (250 g) bittersweet
chocolate, finely chopped

2 Tbsp (25 mL) corn syrup

3 sheets real gold leaf,
for decorating

MAKES 10 SERVINGS

The world's most popular schnapps just gained a cake and this decadent showstopper is ideal for any celebration in need of a little bling. It brings together chocolate and cinnamon—an uncommon but delicious flavor pairing—and creates a devilish match of spicy sweetness, which is then enrobed in a velvety smooth dark chocolate ganache and garnished with flakes of real gold leaf. Simply grand.

PREHEAT OVEN TO 350°F (180°C). Grease and flour two 8-inch (20-cm) round cake pans and line bottoms with parchment paper.

Combine flour, sugar, cocoa, baking powder, and baking soda in a large bowl and make a well in the center. Add mayonnaise, water and Goldschläger to well and stir with a wooden spoon until batter is smooth. Pour batter into prepared pans and bake for 30 to 35 minutes or until toothpick inserted in center comes out clean. Remove from oven and cool in pans for 10 minutes then invert onto racks and cool completely before frosting.

To make the buttercream, place egg yolks and 2 Tbsp (25 mL) sugar in bowl of electric mixer and beat until light and fluffy. Melt chocolate in a small bowl over a *bain marie* (a pot of gently simmering water). Set aside to cool.

Dissolve sugar in water in a small non-stick skillet over medium heat, stirring constantly. Bring to a boil, stop stirring and cook syrup until it reaches 248°F (120°C) on a candy thermometer. Slowly pour syrup over egg mixture while beating on medium speed (being careful not to hit blades of beaters, spinning sugar onto sides of the bowl) until completely incorporated. Add butter, a piece at a time, beating well after each addition until completely incorporated. Stir in melted chocolate and Goldschläger and allow to cool at room temperature until ready to use.

Meanwhile, cut each cake layer in half with a serrated knife, creating 4 layers. Spread Goldschläger buttercream evenly over first 3 layers and top with last cake layer. Use an off-set spatula or knife to smooth the sides. Chill in refrigerator until ready to glaze.

To make the ganache, heat cream in a small saucepan over medium heat until it just comes to a boil. Place chocolate in a medium bowl, pour cream over chocolate and allow to sit for 30 seconds. Stir until smooth. Add corn syrup and stir to combine. Allow mixture to cool until slightly thickened.

Place cake on a wire rack over wax paper and pour over ganache, making sure to completely cover top and sides.

Break up gold leaf into small pieces with two forks in a small bowl. Hold cake on an angle and sprinkle sides with gold pieces. Store in refrigerator in a closed container for up to 4 days.

Carrot Cake

½ cup (125 mL) Baileys

½ cup (125 mL) Kahlúa

2 Tbsp (25 mL) Goldschläger

COMBINE BAILEY'S, Kahlúa and Goldschläger in a cocktail shaker filled with ice and shake vigorously. Strain into shot glasses and garnish with a piece of gold leaf, if desired. MAKES 10 SHOOTERS.

GILDING THE LILY

To be edible, gold leaf must be between 22 and 24 karat. It has no taste and can be used to decorate desserts, pastries, chocolates or one very fancy meatloaf. The leaf itself is manufactured by hammering solid gold into a gossamer-thin sheet. It needs to be handled carefully, ideally with a sable brush or tweezers, as it can dissolve from the moisture of your hand. It can be purchased in sheets at art supply stores, or already prepared at gourmet cooking stores.

Cranberry and Almond Irish Whiskey Cake

CAKE

1 cup (250 mL) dried cranberries

1 cup (250 mL) raisins

2 Tbsp (25 mL) grated lemon zest

2 Tbsp (25 mL) grated orange zest

1 cup (250 mL) Irish whiskey

¾ cup (175 mL) butter, softened

1 cup (250 mL) packed brown sugar

3 eggs, separated

1½ cups (375 mL) cake-and-pastry flour

1 tsp (5 mL) baking powder

½ tsp (2 mL) salt

½ tsp (2 mL) cinnamon

½ tsp (2 mL) nutmeg

¼ tsp (1 mL) ground cloves

¾ cup (175 mL) chopped almonds

IRISH WHIPPED CREAM

2 cups (500 mL) heavy cream (38%)

¼ cup (50 mL) Irish Cream liqueur

¼ cup (50 mL) confectioner's sugar

½ tsp (2 mL) cinnamon

MAKES 12 SERVINGS

At nearly 80 proof this is one feisty confection. The addition of whiskey makes it unbelievably moist and gives it boozy super powers, meaning an almost indefinite shelf life. If you have time, make this up to a month ahead of time and bathe it with ¼ cup (50 mL) of whiskey once a week. By the time St. Paddy's Day rolls around it'll be perfectly pickled.

COMBINE CRANBERRIES, raisins, citrus zest and ½ cup (125 mL) whiskey in a small bowl. Cover with plastic wrap and let sit at room temperature for at least 3 hours or overnight.

Preheat oven to 350°F (170°C). Butter and flour a 9-inch (23-cm) bundt pan.

Cream butter and sugar together until light and fluffy. Add egg yolks, one at a time, beating well after each addition, until completely incorporated.

In a separate bowl, whisk together flour, baking powder, salt, cinnamon, nutmeg and cloves. Add to egg mixture and beat quickly until combined. Stir in cranberry mixture.

In another clean bowl, whisk egg whites until stiff. Fold into batter with almonds and pour into prepared pan. Bake for 45 to 60 minutes or until toothpick inserted in center comes out clean. Cool completely on wire rack. Serve with Irish whipped cream.

To make the whipped cream, combine cream, liqueur, sugar and cinnamon in a large bowl and beat with electric mixer until soft peaks form.

Black Velvet

3 oz champagne

3 oz Guinness

POUR EQUAL AMOUNTS OF CHAMPAGNE and Guinness into champagne flutes and sip. You won't believe how good this is.

Tipsy Chocolate Truffles

1 lb (500 g) semi-sweet chocolate, finely chopped

1 cup (250 mL) heavy cream (38%)

1 tsp (5 mL) vanilla

2 Tbsp (25 mL) liqueur of your choice

2 Tbsp (25 mL) butter, cut into small pieces

Confectioner's sugar or cocoa

MAKES 48 TRUFFLES

Truffles are one of the most decadent and versatile desserts you can make. Once you discover how easy they are you'll need to invent a myth to explain the source of your skills. We suggest something involving a Belgian monastery and years of seclusion. Truffles can be flavored with any spirit or liqueur, but some of our favorites include crème de menthe, Cointreau and icewine.

PLACE CHOCOLATE IN GLASS or stainless steel bowl. Stir cream, vanilla and liqueur in a saucepan over medium heat until barely simmering. Pour cream over chocolate and let sit for 30 seconds. Stir gently until smooth. Add butter a piece at a time and stir constantly until incorporated. Transfer to a shallow baking dish. Cover and refrigerate until firm. Use a teaspoon to roll chocolate into balls, then coat in confectioner's sugar or cocoa powder.

White Russian

1 oz vodka

1 oz Kahlúa

4 oz milk

COMBINE VODKA, Kahlúa and milk in an old-fashioned glass filled with ice and garnish with a maraschino cherry, if desired.

FORAGING FOR TRUFFLES

Truffles can also be rolled in shredded coconut or finely chopped nuts. To really wow the crowd, flavor your truffle mixture with Chambord and form the truffle around a whole fresh raspberry.

Chocolate Chip Banana Bread *with* Kahlúa Ice Cream

KAHLÚA ICE CREAM

3 cups (750 mL) vanilla ice cream

3 Tbsp (45 mL) Kahlúa

¼ cup (50 mL) chocolate-covered espresso beans (optional)

BANANA BREAD

2 cups (500 mL) all-purpose flour

1 cup (250 mL) granulated sugar

1½ tsp (7 mL) baking soda

1 tsp (5 mL) baking powder

Pinch salt

3 small bananas, mashed

¾ cup (175 mL) mayonnaise (full-fat is best)

3 oz (75 g) bittersweet chocolate, chopped

MAKES 8 SERVINGS

The next time you need to bond with the leaders of tomorrow get yourselves together in the kitchen and create this little gem for the family. This dessert couldn't be easier to make—right down to the use of mayo instead of eggs and oil. If you need to bring this more into the adult realm, drizzle some crème de banane on the plate prior to serving.

ALLOW ICE CREAM TO SIT at room temperature for 30 minutes. Stir in Kahlúa and chopped espresso beans (if using) until smooth. Return to freezer for at least 4 hours, or until firm.

Preheat oven to 325°F (160°C).

Whisk flour, sugar, baking soda, baking powder and salt in a large bowl until combined. Add bananas, mayonnaise and ¼ cup (50 mL) water and beat with a wooden spoon until smooth. Fold in chopped chocolate and pour into loaf pan. Bake for 1 hour or until toothpick inserted in center comes out clean. Cool completely before serving.

Cut banana bread into slices and arrange on plates with a scoop of Kahlúa ice cream. Top with chocolate sauce and whipped cream, if desired.

Chocolate Monkey

1 scoop chocolate ice cream

1 oz chocolate syrup

½ oz crème de banane liqueur

1 oz crème de cacao

4 oz chocolate milk or white milk

PLACE ICE CREAM IN A PILSNER GLASS and top with chocolate syrup, liqueurs and milk. Serve with a straw.

THE CLASSICS

COOKING WITH BOOZE

Red Wine Marinara Sauce

3 Tbsp (45 mL) extra virgin olive oil

1 onion, finely chopped

2 cloves garlic, minced

2 28-oz cans (796-mL) crushed tomatoes

½ cup (125 mL) Valpolicella or Cabernet Franc

½ cup (125 mL) chopped fresh basil

¼ cup (50 mL) chopped fresh oregano

Salt

Freshly ground black pepper

MAKES 4 CUPS (1 L)

Marinara is the starting point for a multitude of dishes: add ground beef or pork and serve over spaghetti; toss in clams, mussels and shrimp and serve over linguini; or spoon over chicken Parmesan. Canned plum tomatoes are best because they're picked and processed at their peak, unleashing the freshest tomato flavor. You may be tempted to get heavy-handed with the wine but do be careful. When the sauce reduces, the flavors concentrate and you still want to be able to taste the tomatoes. Hmmm, when did we become the Temperance League?

HEAT OIL IN LARGE STOCKPOT over medium heat. Add onion and garlic and sauté until onion is translucent, about 10 minutes. Add tomatoes and wine. Bring to a simmer, reduce heat to low and simmer uncovered for 1 hour, or until thickened slightly. Right before serving add basil and oregano and season to taste with salt and pepper.

Winter Warmer

2½ cups (625 mL) Valpolicella

⅓ cup (75 mL) Grand Marnier

1 Tbsp (15 mL) granulated sugar

½ cup (125 mL) fresh orange juice

½ cup (125 mL) fresh lemon juice

1 cinnamon stick

COMBINE WINE, Grand Marnier, sugar, orange juice, lemon juice and cinnamon in a medium saucepan and heat gently over medium heat. Pour into specialty coffee glasses and garnish with an orange twist, if desired. MAKES 6 SERVINGS.

Best-Ever Beef Bourguignon

The best cut of beef to use for this dish is chuck, with its high fat content. If you're faced with packages of meat that say only "stewing," look for nicely marbled pieces. Simmering even the toughest cut of meat in a nice big burgundy for 2 hours will result in a gorgeous and tender stew. Although, to be honest, simmering anything in a burgundy for a few hours is always a great place to start and frees up much-needed time for the really important things—like calculating how many extra bottles you'll need to feed a hungry table. (One per person should suffice.)

TOSS BEEF WITH SALT AND PEPPER. Heat oil in large Dutch oven over high heat until smoking hot. Sauté beef until seared on all sides and well browned. Be sure not to overcrowd pan and work in batches if needed. Remove beef from pan and set aside.

Reduce heat to medium-high, add onions and sauté until golden, about 8 minutes. Sprinkle flour over onions, stir and cook for an additional 1 to 2 minutes. Deglaze pan with wine, stirring to ensure you get all the yummy golden bits stuck on the bottom of pan. Add beef, carrots and bay leaves. Fold rosemary and thyme together into a tight bundle and tie with butcher's twine. Add to pot with garlic. Reduce heat, cover and simmer for 2 hours or until beef is fork tender. Remove herbs and discard. Serve over boiled potatoes.

Burgundy Blazer

BEAUJOLAIS AND CÔTES DE NUIT are two of the most popular red wines from the Burgundy region of France but Beaune and Pommard are also notable appellations. Both Pinot Noir and Gamay grapes are grown in Burgundy, with Gamay producing a lighter and fruitier wine, like those from the Beaujolais region.

2 lb (1 kg) chuck, cubed

2 tsp (10 mL) salt

1 tsp (5 mL) freshly ground black pepper

¼ cup (50 mL) vegetable oil

4 onions, thinly sliced

2 Tbsp (25 mL) all-purpose flour

1 bottle (750 mL) red burgundy

6 carrots, coarsely chopped

2 bay leaves

1 sprig fresh rosemary

3 sprigs fresh thyme

1 clove garlic, sliced in half

MAKES 6 SERVINGS

French Onion Soup

6 strips bacon

2 Tbsp (25 mL) butter

3 large sweet onions, halved and thinly sliced

1 cup (250 mL) white Bordeaux or Chardonnay

8 cups (2 L) beef stock

6 sprigs fresh thyme, chopped, plus more for garnish

Salt

Freshly ground black pepper

18 slices baguette, toasted

1½ cups (375 mL) shredded Gruyère

MAKES 6 SERVINGS

What can we say about French onion soup? Sweet onions caramelized in bacon drippings, rich beef stock and that bubbling layer of cheese on top. Comfort in a bowl. You can use any type of sweet onion—Vidalia, white or even red—but the genuine article is yellow Spanish. These onions take on the soup's signature dark color when caramelized and add richness to the broth. Bon appetit.

CRISP BACON IN LARGE STOCKPOT over medium heat. Remove bacon from pan and drain on paper towel. Crumble.

Add butter and onions to pot and cook for 5 minutes or until onions begin to soften. Reduce heat to medium-low and continue to cook for 30 to 40 minutes, until onions are very soft and caramelized. Be careful not to scorch onions.

Add wine, stock and thyme and bring to a simmer over medium heat. Cover and reduce heat to low until ready to serve. Season to taste with salt and pepper.

Preheat broiler.

Ladle soup into bowls. Arrange 3 pieces of toasted baguette on top and sprinkle with cheese and a few bacon pieces. Place bowls on cookie sheet and broil until cheese bubbles and starts to brown around edges. Serve with a sprig of thyme, if desired.

Louis XV (GRANDDADDY OF FRENCH ONION SOUP)

2 oz cognac

½ oz fresh lemon juice

½ oz fresh lime juice

5 oz fresh orange juice

COMBINE COGNAC, lemon juice, lime juice and orange juice in a cocktail shaker filled with ice and shake vigorously. Strain into an old-fashioned glass filled with ice and garnish with an orange wheel, if desired.

Public House Fish 'n' Chips

The leaflet highlighting "Great British Contributions to Culinary Excellence" is pretty thin, but deep-frying is truly a national pastime. As the British know, when you have a good beer batter you can deep-fry anything—Mars bars, sausage, black pudding, tripe, car keys. Straight from our friends across the pond—fish and chips the way Her Majesty intended.

Making great beer batter is simple. Keep the batter as cold as possible and work in small batches. The colder the batter the bigger the reaction when it hits the hot oil, resulting in a lighter, crispier crust. Working with small batches in the fryer helps keep the oil at a consistent temperature, which means the food absorbs less oil.

TO MAKE THE BATTER, combine flour, baking powder, salt, garlic powder, white pepper and cayenne pepper in a large bowl. Slowly whisk in ale until well blended and smooth. Refrigerate until needed.

Preheat oven to 200°F (95°C). Heat oil in a large deep pot or Dutch oven to 350°F (180°C). Line a rimmed cookie sheet with newspaper and place cooling rack on top.

Drain potatoes then lay them on paper towel to soak up excess water. Working in small batches, carefully add sliced potatoes to pot and cook until soft but still pale in appearance, or for about 8 minutes. Remove potatoes and drain on a rack placed on top of prepared cookie sheet. Keep warm in oven.

Ensure oil temperature has returned to 350°F (180°C). Lightly dredge fish in cornstarch and dip in batter, coating evenly. Working in small batches carefully add battered fish to pot and cook until golden, about 6 to 8 minutes, turning once. Remove fish and drain on a rack placed on top of prepared cookie sheet. Keep warm in oven.

Refry potatoes until golden and crisp, about 3 minutes, then drain on newspaper. Serve with sea salt, malt vinegar, lemon wedges and tartar sauce.

To make the tartar sauce, combine tartar sauce ingredients in a medium bowl and refrigerate until ready to serve.

Beer

WHAT ELSE? 3 to try: Boddingtons Pub Ale, Newcastle Brown Ale and Creemore Springs Lager

FISH

2 cups (500 mL) all-purpose flour

1 Tbsp (15 mL) baking powder

1 tsp (5 mL) salt

½ tsp (2 mL) garlic powder

1 tsp (5 mL) white pepper

¼ tsp (1 mL) cayenne pepper

1 12-oz (341-mL) bottle dark ale

1½ lb (750 g) halibut, tilapia or cod fillets

1 cup (250 mL) cornstarch

CHIPS

4 large Russet potatoes, sliced and soaked in water

12 cups (3 L) vegetable oil

TARTAR SAUCE

1 cup (250 mL) mayonnaise

2 Tbsp (25 mL) chopped dill pickle

2 Tbsp (25 mL) fresh lime juice

1 Tbsp (15 mL) Limoncello Di Leva

1 Tbsp (15 mL) wasabi or horseradish

1 tsp (5 mL) lime zest

MAKES 4 SERVINGS

Muffuletta Sandwich

There's nothing small about a muffuletta sandwich. It's the uncontested supreme ruler of the sandwich world. Think of this scaled down version as the slightly more intimate cousin, perfect for satiating the appetites of two hungry romantics.

CUT THE LOAF AROUND THE TOP on an angle to create a bowl and lid. Drizzle olive oil over both the heel and crown of the muffuletta. Set aside the crown. Spread half of the tapenade on the heel and layer with provolone, prosciutto, roasted red peppers, havarti, smoked turkey, red onion, mozzarella, salami and basil. Spread remaining tapenade inside the crown. Replace the crown and use a sturdy breadboard to compress the sandwich. Refrigerate for at least 3 hours or overnight. Slice into quarters.

Belini

1 oz peach purée

Dash grenadine

5 oz chilled sparkling wine

LAYER PEACH PURÉE and grenadine in a champagne flute and top with sparkling wine.

1 small round loaf bread

2 Tbsp (25 mL) olive oil

1¼ cups (300 mL) Cabernet Tapenade (page 32)

3 slices provolone

4 slices prosciutto

¼ cup (50 mL) roasted red peppers (see sidebar page 58)

3 slices havarti

4 slices smoked turkey

½ cup (125 mL) sliced red onion

3 slices buffalo mozzarella

6 slices hot Genoa salami

½ cup (125 mL) fresh basil

Salt

Freshly ground black pepper

MAKES 2–4 SERVINGS

Swiss Fondue

3 Tbsp (45 mL) cornstarch

3 Tbsp (45 mL) kirsch

2 cloves garlic, cut in half

2 cups (500 mL) Chardonnay
or Riesling

3 cups (750 mL) shredded
Emmenthal cheese

3 cups (750 mL) shredded
Gruyère cheese

2 baguettes, cubed

MAKES 4 SERVINGS

Fondue is comfort food at its most civilized. There is something extremely intimate about sharing a hot pot of gooey cheese, and this classic is perfect on a cold winter night with good friends and good wine. (Roaring fire optional.) Serve this fondue with ramekins of kirsch on the side for dipping and remember, tradition dictates that those who lose their bread in the pot drink a shot of kirsch.

Scale the recipe down by half for a romantic evening for two. (Don't scale down the roaring fire.)

MIX CORNSTARCH and kirsch together in a small bowl and set aside. Rub inside of fondue pot with garlic and leave garlic in pot. Set aside.

Add wine to a medium non-stick pot and bring to a gentle simmer over medium-low heat. Slowly add small handfuls of cheese to hot wine, stirring constantly. When all the cheese has melted, stir in cornstarch and kirsch mixture. Pour cheese into fondue pot and serve.

Cherry Bomb

Dash grenadine

Dash kirsch

5 oz champagne

ADD GRENADINE and kirsch to flute and top with champagne.

ON THE SIDE

Keep the heat low and take things slowly. Remember, the Swiss are master clockmakers and very patient people. If the mixture becomes too thick, add small amounts of wine to thin it down. If your fondue separates, dissolve ½ tsp (2 mL) cornstarch in a little wine, warm it slightly and add to the pot. Stir until mixture comes back together.

Guinness Irish Stew

1 cup (250 mL) pearl barley

2 16-oz cans (500-mL) Guinness

10 cups (2.5 L) beef stock

3 lb (1.5 kg) lamb shoulder, cubed

2 tsp (10 mL) salt

¼ cup (50 mL) vegetable oil

½ cup (125 mL) all-purpose flour

2 cups (500 mL)
pearl onions, peeled

4 cloves garlic, minced

3 large carrots, thickly sliced

6 stalks celery, thickly sliced

3 large potatoes,
peeled and cubed

6 sprigs fresh thyme

3 sprigs fresh rosemary

3 bay leaves

Salt

Freshly ground black pepper

MAKES 6–8 SERVINGS

Got a chill? Make a pot of this classic stew and you'll stay warm through to spring. Lamb may not be everyone's thing, but if you're going to substitute that you may as well replace the Guinness with apple juice and serve it in Peter Rabbit bowls.

COMBINE BARLEY, 1 can Guinness and 1½ cups (375 mL) beef stock and cook over medium heat for 20 minutes. Cover and set aside.

Season lamb with salt. Heat oil in large stockpot over medium-high heat, add meat in batches and cook until well browned on all sides. Transfer to large shallow baking dish and toss with flour. Add onions, garlic, carrots and celery to pan and sauté for 3 to 4 minutes. Add remaining can of Guinness and deglaze pan, scraping all the bits from the bottom. Add potatoes, lamb, barley and remaining stock. Fold thyme and rosemary together and tie with butcher's twine. Add to pot with bay leaves and bring to a boil, then reduce heat to low, cover and simmer for 2 to 3 hours or until lamb is fork tender, stirring occasionally.

Remove herbs and season to taste with salt and pepper. Spoon into shallow bowls and serve with thick crusty bread.

Guinness Martini

2 oz vanilla vodka

1 oz espresso

½ oz Tia Maria

½ oz Bailey's

COMBINE VODKA, espresso, Tia Maria and Bailey's in a cocktail shaker filled with ice and shake vigorously. Strain into a chilled martini glass and garnish with an espresso bean, if desired.

Cherries Jubilee

This dessert was first made for Queen Victoria on her Golden Jubilee (50 short years on the British throne) by French chef Auguste Escoffier. Originally this dessert was served in small dishes and flamed individually, sans ice cream, but today it's almost always understood to be a topping for vanilla ice cream. Without ice cream it's really just boozy cherries, and while there is certainly nothing wrong with that, we just think that's called a breakfast cereal topping.

1 Tbsp (15 mL) cornstarch

1 Tbsp (15 mL) granulated sugar

2 cups (500 mL) whole Bing cherries in juice, drained and juice reserved

¼ cup (50 mL) kirsch or cherry brandy

6 large scoops vanilla ice cream

MAKES 6 SERVINGS

DISSOLVE CORNSTARCH and sugar with 3 Tbsp (45 mL) reserved cherry juice in a small bowl. Pour remaining cherry juice into medium skillet and warm over medium heat. Add cornstarch mixture and continue heating until slightly thickened. Add cherries and heat until warmed though. Pour on kirsch and flambé.

Place ice cream in large wine goblets and spoon over cherries.

Cherry Coke Float

2 scoops vanilla ice cream

1½ oz cherry brandy

6 oz cola

PLACE ICE CREAM and cherry brandy in pilsner glass and slowly pour in cola. Serve with two straws and a cherry.

Crêpes Suzette

Sometimes the best things to happen in the kitchen are mistakes. (Just ask David.) This recipe was created by 14-year-old French sous chef Henri Charpentier when he accidentally set his crêpe sauce on fire while serving the Prince of Wales, Britain's future King Edward VII. Asked what he called his creation Charpentier replied, "Crêpes Princesse," but the prince asked if he'd dedicate the dish to the daughter of one of his guests and so Crêpes Suzette was born.

FOR THE CRÊPES, whisk together flour, milk, eggs, vanilla and melted butter until smooth. Heat a little vegetable oil in a medium non-stick skillet over medium heat. Pour in some batter (about ⅓ cup/75 mL per crêpe) and rotate skillet so a thin layer of batter covers the bottom. Fry until brown on underside and dry on top. Flip crêpe and cook for another 20 seconds or until lightly browned. Transfer crêpe to a plate and continue until all batter is used. Fold crêpes in half and then in half again to make triangles. Set aside.

To make the sauce, melt butter in a large skillet over medium heat. Add sugar and grated orange zest and cook until caramelized. Pour in orange juice and simmer for 2 to 3 minutes until reduced slightly. Add Grand Marnier, orange segments and crêpes to the pan and coat with sauce. Drizzle over cognac and flambé. Place 2 crêpes on each plate and spoon over sauce.

Rolls Royce

2 oz cognac

2 oz Cointreau

2 oz orange juice

COMBINE COGNAC, Cointreau and orange juice in a cocktail shaker filled with ice and shake vigorously. Strain into a chilled martini glass.

CRÊPES

1½ cups (375 mL) all-purpose flour, sifted

1½ cups (375 mL) milk

2 eggs

1 tsp (5 mL) vanilla

2 Tbsp (25 mL) melted butter, cooled

SAUCE

3 Tbsp (45 mL) butter

¼ cup (50 mL) granulated sugar

1 Tbsp (15 mL) grated orange zest

1½ cups (375 mL) fresh orange juice

¼ cup (50 mL) Grand Marnier

1 cup (250 mL) orange segments

2 Tbsp (25 mL) cognac

MAKES 4 SERVINGS

THE CLASSICS

Poached Pears *with* Mascarpone Cream

PEARS

1 lemon

1 orange

1 bottle (750 mL) Zinfandel

8 cups (2 L) water

½ cup (125 mL) honey

1-inch (2.5-cm) piece
fresh ginger, sliced

½ tsp (2 mL) cloves

1 vanilla bean, sliced in half

6 firm pears, peeled

MASCARPONE CREAM

1½ cups (375 mL)
mascarpone cheese

3 Tbsp (45 mL) granulated sugar

2 Tbsp (25 mL) heavy
cream (38%)

2 Tbsp (25 mL) Bailey's

1 tsp (5 mL) vanilla

½ cup (125 mL) pistachios,
shelled and chopped

MAKES 6 SERVINGS

In the dog house? Looking to impress the neighbors? These crowd-stoppers are your ticket to redemption and will instantly elevate your culinary prowess from capable to enviable. Zinfandel is our wine of choice for this dessert. Its deep fruity flavors and peppery notes complement the buttery nature of the pears but Shiraz is also a good choice. Use the firmest pears you can find.

REMOVE RIND FROM LEMON and orange with a vegetable peeler then cut in half and juice. Combine rind, juice, wine, water, honey, ginger, cloves and vanilla bean in a large stockpot and bring to a gentle simmer over medium-high heat. Reduce heat to low (just below a simmer). Add pears, cover and poach until tender but not mushy, anywhere from 15 to 30 minutes depending on size, ripeness and variety. (An inserted knife should still meet some resistance.)

Gently transfer pears to a large non-reactive bowl and pour over poaching liquid, just to cover. Cover and refrigerate for several hours or overnight.

Strain remaining poaching liquid and return to saucepan. Cook over high heat until a syrupy consistency is reached and liquid thinly coats the back of a spoon. Chill until ready to serve.

Meanwhile, cream mascarpone, sugar and vanilla together in a medium bowl. Stir in pistachio nuts and transfer to a piping bag fitted with a round tip.

Slice the top off each pear and use an apple corer or paring knife to hollow out a 1-inch (2.5-cm) wide cavity. Fill the cavity with the mascarpone cream mixture, place top back on pears and stand in individual serving bowls. Spoon syrup around pears and serve.

Poire Noir

2 oz Xanté Poire au Cognac

½ oz Cointreau

6 oz ginger ale

Splash cranberry juice

FILL A COLLINS GLASS WITH ICE, add Xanté, Cointreau, ginger ale and cranberry juice and garnish with a pear slice, if desired.

Tiramisù

½ cup (125 mL) espresso
or strong coffee

¼ cup (50 mL) brandy
or dark rum

2 Tbsp (25 mL) Grand Marnier

4 egg yolks

¼ cup (50 mL) granulated sugar

2 egg whites

2 cups (500 mL) mascarpone
cheese

30 small ladyfingers
(Savoiardi are best)

6 oz (175 g) bittersweet
chocolate, finely chopped

6 large wine goblets

MAKES 6 SERVINGS

This classic Italian dessert translates to "pick-me-up," probably because of the espresso- and booze-soaked ladyfingers. No matter what you call it, it's delicious. Traditionally, only Italian brandy is used but, on a suggestion from Sophia Loren, we also added some Grand Marnier. We think Sophia's got it right.

COMBINE ESPRESSO, brandy and Grand Marnier and set aside.

Whisk egg yolks and sugar together in stainless steel bowl over a *bain-marie* (a pot of gently simmering water) until thick ribbons fall from whisk. Remove from heat and allow to cool for 5 minutes.

Meanwhile, beat egg whites until stiff peaks form.

Fold mascarpone into egg yolk mixture in 2 batches then fold mascarpone-egg yolk mixture into egg whites. Set aside.

Dip ladyfingers into espresso mixture and line wine goblets or large martini glasses, reserving 6 biscuits for later. Fill goblets with half the mascarpone mixture and sprinkle with half the chocolate. Top each glass with a reserved ladyfinger and more mascarpone and chocolate. Refrigerate for at least 3 hours or until ready to serve—overnight is best.

White Heather

¾ oz scotch

¾ oz crème de banane

¾ oz crème de cacao

1½ oz milk

COMBINE SCOTCH, liqueurs and milk in a cocktail shaker filled with ice and shake vigorously. Strain into a chilled martini glass and sprinkle with nutmeg, if desired.

GET-TOGETHERS

NEW YEAR'S EVE TAPAS MENU
December 31st **162**

BURNS SUPPER
WITH SCOTCH SAMPLING
January 25th **164**

ST. PATRICK'S DAY
March 17th **168**

MOTHER'S DAY BRUNCH
The 2nd Sunday in May **170**

MIDSUMMER'S NIGHT PICNIC
June 20th–July 7th **172**

COOKING WITH BOOZE

New Year's Eve Tapas Menu

If we have to listen to one more person complain about how overrated New Year's is we might have to scream. Not because New Year's isn't overrated but because screaming draws attention and attention draws a crowd and crowds make parties and parties make people happy. What we're getting at here is to forget about finding the best New Year's party in the city and have it yourself, at home, with the best group of people you can find. New Year's is a time when you get to indulge. Splurge on a few good bottles of champagne and stock your refrigerator with a selection of seafood such as lobster, crab claws and shrimp. They only need a little steaming and some drawn garlic butter to make quick crowd-pleasing nibbles.

The Menu

Oyster Shooters (page 47)

Beer Crostini with Figs and Gorgonzola (page 56)

Apricot and Vanilla Chicken Baskets (page 50)

Killa Crab Cakes (page 39)

Bloody Caesar Steamed Mussels (page 43)

Tipsy Chocolate Truffles (page 141)

Setting the Mood

LIGHTING, LIGHTING, LIGHTING. If all your common-area lights aren't already on dimmer switches, get thee to a hardware store and install some immediately. Nothing makes people more uncomfortable than floodlights highlighting their pasty winter skin. A fireplace creates instant ambiance. No fireplace? You could go out and buy one of those DVDs that you plug into your machine and have your guests sit in front of your TV watching a fire burn, but, to be honest, we don't suggest this. Better to light as many candles as you can find (please be safe, our insurance rates are already astronomical) and spread them evenly around the room or group them on a mantel or credenza.

A selection of noisemakers, horns and streamers is a must. Cluster them in a bowl or arrange in a collection of drinking glasses and allow people to help themselves when the midnight countdown begins. Forgo the party hats.

The Drink

IT'S NEW YEAR'S EVE so champagne is definitely in order. Have a selection of liqueurs on hand and have your guests create their own champagne cocktails. To get you started there's the Kir Royale (page 37), the French Kiss (page 62) and the Cherry Bomb (page 152).

The Music

GROOVE ARMADA—"BEST OF GROOVE ARMADA"

Thank gawd the Groove Armada hipsters came out with a "Best of" CD so we don't have the difficult task of picking a favorite from their previous recordings. The UK dance act packs 12 of their best upbeat and downbeat tunes into this offering and it's perfect for getting the party going. Tracks like the bootie-slappin' "I See You Baby" are what parties are all about.

PARLIAMENT—"THE BEST OF PARLIAMENT: GIVE UP THE FUNK"

No party's complete without a dose of George Clinton and the crazy kids of Parliament. This 14-track dance disk is just enough to satisfy your funkadelic cravings and hits like "Give Up the Funk" and "Up for the Down Stroke" will have your guests grinding their heels into your carpet and shaking their hips before the dessert plates are cleared.

VARIOUS ARTISTS—"VERVE REMIXED"

This first disk in a series of classic jazz tunes reinvented by the world's best DJs is still the best of the lot. Tricky ingeniously takes on Nina Simone's "See-line Woman," and Richard Dorfmeister adds a whole new bass-line and life to Willie Bobo's "Spanish Grease," among ten other equally stellar mixes. If this CD doesn't put you in the mood to party, there's little hope.

Burns Supper *with* Scotch Sampling

Robert Burns is Scotland's national poet and author of "Auld Lang Syne," "The "Selkirk Grace" and "To a Mouse"—the poem that inspired Steinbeck's classic Of Mice and Men. *Burns Suppers are a long-standing tradition and one of two major Scottish celebrations, the other being Hogmanay (New Year's Eve). Burns Suppers are steeped in protocol, but hosting a simple night for close friends and family is well within the spirit (as it were). Burns Night is celebrated on January 25, Burns's birthday.*

Hosting a scotch sampling is a great way to expose your senses to a myriad of single malt whiskies. To avoid breaking the bank, ask each of your guests to bring a bottle. Guidelines are provided on page 165 for what to get, why and when to serve.

The Menu

SCOTLAND'S TRADITIONAL CUISINE is not always the most appetizing fare for modern palates. A traditional supper would typically consist of cock'a'leekie soup, haggis, roasted neeps (rutabaga and parsnips) and chappit tatties (mashed potatoes). We've created our own special appetizer that's perfectly matched for an evening of scotch sampling and the rest of the menu nods in acknowledgement to our friends across the pond.

Lox, Stock and Capers (page 34)

Carrot, Ginger and Drambuie Soup (page 59)

Braised Lamb Shanks with Sherry-Poached Figs (page 93)

Cherries Jubilee (page 155)

Setting the Mood

SCOTLAND MUST SURELY have one of the most internationally identifiable cultural brands we know of, which makes your work here easy. Anything tartan is a good place to start—rent a kilt, fill urns with fresh heather and provide some printed versions of Burns's poetry for your guests to peruse.

A traditional Burns supper contains a number of toasts and addresses, including the 18th-century sexually charged "Toasts to the Lassies" and "Reply from the Lassies." Personally, we think this is an excellent opportunity to point out some of the better features of either sex! Lastly, for your everyday enjoyment, Burns wrote what could be considered the most direct grace ever written. The Scots are generally not ones to mince words.

THE SELKIRK GRACE

This grace, written by Burns around 1795 or 1796, is a great example of Scottish pragmatism at its best. This traditional grace should be said as your guests sit down for supper. The rough translation for this grace would simply be "Thanks for the food, we're hungry and lucky to have it."

The Scotch Sampling

Aperitif—Lowland, top quality blends or Light Highland Malts

Served with Supper—Highland Malts, Speysides

After Supper—Island Malts

MAKE YOUR SAMPLING as interactive as possible and have your guests introduce the scotch they brought.

Provide your guests with small notebooks to take notes. If you have the time (and talent), personalize these for the occasion. Encourage your guests to discuss the merits of each scotch as they sample but remember it all comes down to personal preference. Refer to the section "Scotch 101" on page 166 for regional flavor notes and page 167 for a sample tasting notes format.

The Music

VARIOUS ARTISTS—"SCOTLAND THE BRAVE"

For centuries the bagpipes led the way into battle for Scotland's armies, instilling heroism into troops and fear into the enemy. This disk will have your guests poking each other with pointy spears in no time, to the traditional pipe and drum marches recorded by the world's best pipe bands.

FRANZ FERDINAND—"FRANZ FERDINAND"

This Glasgow foursome's pop-rock entry into the music biz is full of air guitar-worthy songs and fluffy toe-tapping hits like "Take Me Out" and "Cheating On You." A worthy disk from start to finish, you'll find your CD player won't want to spit this one out, so indulge yourself and crank it up loud for the best effect. The neighbors will thank you for it, we promise.

THE SELKIRK GRACE

Some hae meat and canna eat,
and some wad eat that want it,
but we hae meat and we can eat,
and sae the Lord be thankit.

SCOTCHES

LOWLAND MALTS

Glenkinchie (10 year)

LIGHT HIGHLAND MALTS

Sheepdip (8 year)

Glenmorangie (10 year)

FULL HIGHLAND MALTS

Oban (14 year)

Glen Ord (12 year)

LIGHT SPEYSIDE MALTS

The Glenlivet (12 year)

Cardhu (12 year)

FULL SPEYSIDE MALTS

The Balvenie (10 year)

Glenrothes (12 year)

ISLAND AND ISLAY MALTS

Talisker (10 year)

Scapa Single Orkney Malt (14 year)

Lagavulin (10 year)

Scotch 101

There are two types of scotches: single malt and blended. The latter consists of the various blends of the former, which allows the distillery to tune flavors. Single-malt scotches are generally considered to be better quality, but don't dismiss the blends just yet. Johnny Walker Blue, a famed blend, is perhaps one of the most buttery, smooth and delicate scotches widely available.

SINGLE MALTS

Scotland is divided into two scotch-producing regions, Highland and Lowland, and each has characteristically different flavors. Highland scotches are generally peaty in flavor, a characteristic brought about by the burning of peat moss to dry the malted barley. Lowland scotches, on the other hand, are lighter in color and, to the undistinguished palate, smoother and more enjoyable. The lighter the scotch, the less peaty the flavor.

LOWLAND MALT SCOTCHES

Lowland scotches are a good place to start for the novice whisky drinker. They are delicately flavored with honey notes and fruits, including apple. Lowland malts can be served "neat" as an aperitif.

HIGHLAND MALT SCOTCHES

The Highland region is Scotland's largest scotch-producing region and consists of two sub-regions: Speyside and Island. Generally, the Highland malts are best served after dinner, although a light Highland malt—comparable to a Lowland malt—can be served as an aperitif.

Speyside is the Highland sub-region located around the River Spey. It produces whiskies that tend to be clean, with subtle honey-like notes. Speyside malts are perfect for after dinner, and blended-whisky drinkers will find them the most familiar.

Island is the Highland sub-region comprising the islands that surround Scotland's northern tip and east coast. Highland and Island malts are typically full bodied and heavily peated. Approach these with caution since it takes an acquired taste to realize their subtleties. Island scotches cover a collection of islands so each region can again be sub-categorized: The Orkneys, Isle of Skye, Mull, Jura and Islay—yours to discover.

SCOTCH:			RATING:	
APPEARANCE	AROMA	FLAVOR	FINISH	OTHER NOTES
REVIEWED BY:				

SCOTCH:			RATING:	
APPEARANCE	AROMA	FLAVOR	FINISH	OTHER NOTES
REVIEWED BY:				

SCOTCH:			RATING:	
APPEARANCE	AROMA	FLAVOR	FINISH	OTHER NOTES
REVIEWED BY:				

St. Patrick's Day

The Menu

Beer Crostini with Figs and Gorgonzola (page 56)

Guinness Irish Stew (page 154) in mini bread bowls

Cranberry and Almond Irish Whiskey Cake (page 138)

Setting the Mood

What would this book be without an ode to St. Patrick's Day? We suggest taking the 18th off. And while it's tough to class up this act, here are the rules for a rather more sophisticated evening—you might not like them.

1. IF YOU'RE GOING TO DECORATE IN GREEN make it as natural as possible by using fresh shamrocks. Place a Blarney stone at the front door and invite your guests to kiss it as they enter. Horseshoes and little pots of gold coins (the chocolate sort) also work well. And order a couple leprechauns online to man the bar.

2. Don't force your guests to wear green. Nothing is more obnoxious than a host opening the door and judging the attire of his guests. Instead, greet your guests with festive green derby hats. (You've got to have some fun!)

3. Get the whole family involved. Make the kids the official photographers, complete with press credentials and fedoras. Five disposable cameras will provide ample blackmail material for the coming year.

4. As a parting gift, wrap up small boxes of Pot of Gold chocolates to give your guests.

5. And last but not least, no green beer. Instead, serve Irish beer like Guinness, Kilkenny, Harp, Smithwicks, Beamish, Caffrey's—heck we'll even accept Keith's India Pale Ale (IPA) which is brewed in Nova Scotia—but if your friends are gullible enough tell them the "I" in IPA stands for Irish.

The Drink

BEER IS THE OBVIOUS CHOICE (and not a bad one) but for some additional sophistication try Black Velvets (page 138).

Depending on the size of the function, a keg might be the better option and since college may have been a while ago here's a keg refresher course:

1. Clean garbage can—add keg first then fill with ice.

2. Let keg settle for at least an hour before tapping.

3. Pressurize the keg, then let it settle again for at least 30 minutes.

No one wants to look at a trashcan filled with a keg (not even a clean one) so cover it with a tablecloth and create a "drunk" dummy out of old clothes. Sit the dummy on top and attach the draft hose to his hand—voilà, you have an instant bartender. Top with a green derby hat and you're done.

The Music

THE CLANCY BROTHERS WITH TOMMY MAKEM— "COME FILL YOUR GLASS WITH US"

The album that made the Clancy clan a household name in the late '50s is still a classic and as the title suggests, it's perfect for tossing back a few pints. With such ditties as "Whiskey You're the Devil," "Finnigan's Wake" (the song that inspired James Joyce's novel) and "A Jug of Punch" you'll be singing and dancing in the kitchen till the wee hours of the morning.

GREAT BIG SEA—"SEA OF NO CARES"

The boys from The Rock maintain their Celtic flavor on this disk but turn things up a notch with a more electric sound. Accordion, mandola and bodhran still shine through on the lively folk tune "The Scolding Wife," and their ability to keep things upbeat and generously positive is exactly why dear old St. Paddy would approve.

THE THRILLS—"SO MUCH FOR THE CITY"

This Dublin quintet, with a sound like The Monkees meet The Beatles, mix their west coast infatuation with head-bopping harmonies to create a disk that delivers all the way through. Infectious tunes like "Big Sur" and "Don't Steal Our Sun" will have your crowd singing along in no time.

Mother's Day Brunch

Give your little matriarch the royal treatment. Start her day with a private wake-up call complete with Sparkling Wine with Mixed Berries, morning coffee and the Sunday paper served in bed. A bud vase with a fresh gerbera daisy is a nice touch. Include a handmade invitation to join the rest of the family for brunch. While the guest of honor gets ready, greet your other guests with flutes of Sparkling Wine with Mixed Berries. When mother arrives a standing ovation is also very appropriate.

The Menu

Sparkling Wine with Mixed Berries (page 22)

Coddled Eggs with Jägermeister and Brie (page 28)

Sticky Bacon (page 26)

Coconut Cake with Godiva Buttercream (page 134)

The Attire

SHIRTS AND TIES ALL ROUND. Well, except for the ladies.

Setting the Mood

SCENTED CANDLES and fresh flowers are the order of the day—the bigger and brighter the better. Sunflowers, gerbera daisies and white, yellow or pink roses are all good choices.

Nothing makes someone feel more like royalty than being the object of a toast. Traditionally, this would be the domain of the eldest son, but to take the pressure off, select the most appropriate person to introduce and call the toast, and have everyone address his or her most memorable moment with mom.

The Drink

Pitchers of Perfect Caesars (page 43)

or Royal Mimosas (page 16)

The Music

PAUL ANKA—"ROCK SWINGS"

Canada's legendary crooner sings and swings his heart out on this 14-track album that features classic anthems like Nirvana's "Smells Like Teen Spirit" and Survivor's "Eye of the Tiger." A great album to crank loud on your stereo or equally effective as soft background music for a mellow brunch. You'll recognize the lyrics but little else. Anka's inventiveness is one of the reasons he's been able to last five decades in the biz.

NORAH JONES—"FEELS LIKE HOME"

Critics of Ms. Jones like to ask the question, "Is it really jazz?" Well, it doesn't really matter when you sound this good. The follow-up to her debut album showcases a more mature and determined singer/songwriter. Her sweet whispering vocals and the toe-tappin' duet with Dolly Parton are just two reasons to own this album.

RAY CHARLES—"GENIUS LOVES COMPANY"

On his last recordings Charles teamed up with other greats like Gladys Knight, James Taylor and Diana Krall, and this disk reminds us what an utterly smooth lyrical executor he can be. He's in fine form on tracks like "Hey Girl," the aching duet with Michael MacDonald, and the truly inspired "Crazy Love" with Van Morrison. At least he left on a high note.

Midsummer's Night Picnic

Summer is about romance and stars and the best way to bring these together is a Midsummer's Night picnic for two. Timing is important so dust off the almanac—a new moon has a powerful impact.

The Menu

Strawberries, Sambuca and Black Pepper (page 37)

Roasted Red Pepper Gazpacho (page 58)

Muffuletta Sandwich (page 151)

Tipsy Chocolate Truffles (page 141)

Location, Location, Location

WHEN HUNTING FOR THE IDEAL SPOT for your picnic, look for a venue with an unobstructed view of the sky on at least one side. Hillsides, escarpments or bluffs are ideal and typically offer intimacy. For the urbanites who can't exactly take mass transit to a meadow, make it a rooftop with a view, and to ensure it remains intimate, bribe the Super with a bottle of wine.

The Attire

TRADITIONAL "SUMMER WHITES" in light cotton or linen and shades of white and off-white.

Setting the Mood

A LANTERN IS A NECESSITY. After all, you need to see what you're eating. Hang it from a tree branch or set it on the ground.

Bring the stars to you by illuminating the shady areas nearby. Place a tea light in a brown sandwich bag with the top rolled down. Add a rock to keep it anchored and have some water handy, just in case.

Bring a plush blanket and a few throw pillows to make things really comfy.

The Drink

Belinis (page 151)

The Music

BARRY WHITE—"ALL-TIME GREATEST HITS"

Obvious? Maybe. Appropriate? Absolutely. Mr. White's baritone bass can set the mood for a romantic evening in 2.3 seconds flat and this 20-song CD includes all his chart toppers from between 1973 and 1979. Steamy tunes like "Never, Never Gonna Give You Up," "Can't Get Enough of Your Love, Babe" and "You're My First, My Last, My Everything" will have you and your date out of your restrictive clothing in no time.

VARIOUS ARTISTS—"GREAT LADIES OF JAZZ"

Soft and sultry tracks by the likes of Holiday, Simone, Washington and Fitzgerald come together on this compilation and absolutely beg to be played on a hot summer night under the stars. Lay down a blanket, pop the champagne and let songs like "I Loves You, Porgy" and "Deed I Do" transport you to another time and place.

OUTKAST—"SPEAKERBOXXX/THE LOVE BELOW"

Andre 3000's "The Love Below" (one-half of this double CD) is about as sexy a mood as you can set. His funk-soul-jazz vocals coupled with his propensity for love songs like "Happy Valentine's Day" and "Prototype" will provide the perfect lubricant for a midsummer night under a wide open sky. This album is the reason they make cars with backseats.

Index of Alcohol

ABSINTHE (THE GREEN FAIRY)
Flavor notes: herbal, licorice
Main source: wormwood, herbs
Alcohol content: 70%
Substitution: anisette liqueur,
Pernod

ALIZÉ (GOLD, RED, WILD, BLEU)
Flavor notes: passion fruit and
other fruits
Main source: cognac, fruit juices
Alcohol content: 15%
Substitution: combine cognac or
brandy and orange liqueur

AMARETTO
Flavor notes: almond,
maraschino cherry, marzipan
Main source: alcohol,
caramelized sugar, apricot nuts,
fruits
Alcohol content: 28%
Substitution: combine brandy or
cognac and almond extract

AMARETTO CREAM LIQUEUR
Flavor notes: almond,
maraschino cherry
Main source: amaretto, cream
Alcohol: 17%
Substitution: combine amaretto
and cream

AMARULA
Flavor notes: strawberry-like
sweet fruit
Main source: marula fruit,
cream
Alcohol: 17%
Substitution: none

ANISETTE/ANISEED LIQUEUR
Flavor notes: licorice
Main source: anise
Alcohol content: 25-40%
Substitution: Pernod, sambuca,
ouzo, absinthe

APPLE LIQUEUR
Flavor notes: ripe apple
Main source: alcohol, apples
Alcohol content: 20%
Substitution: Calvados

APRICOT BRANDY
Flavor notes: apricot, caramel
Main source: brandy, apricots
Alcohol content: 24%
Substitution: combine brandy
with peach or orange liqueur

ARMAGNAC
Flavor notes: fruity, floral,
woody
Main source: white wine
Alcohol content: 40%
Substitution: brandy, cognac

BAILEY'S IRISH CREAM (SEE IRISH CREAM
LIQUEUR)

BEER
ALE
Flavor notes: malty, hoppy,
full-bodied
Main source: malt and/or
cereal
Alcohol content: 4–6%
Substitution: lager

BOCK
Flavor notes: heavy, strong,
pronounced alcohol
Main source: malt and/or cereal
Alcohol content: 5-8%
Substitution: stout

LAGER
Flavor notes: bright, light
bodied
Main source: malt and/or
cereal
Alcohol content: 4–6%
Substitution: pilsner

LAMBIC (SPONTANEOUSLY FERMENTED
BEER ONLY FROM BELGIUM)
Flavor notes: sour, usually
fruit flavored (cherry, peach,
raspberry)
Main source: malt and/or
cereal
Alcohol content: 4–6%
Substitution: none

MALT LIQUOR (US TERM MEANING ANY
BEER CONTAINING MORE THAN 5%
ALCOHOL)
Flavor notes: various
Main source: malt and/or cereal
Alcohol content: 5%+
Substitution: any beer over 5%

PILSNER
Flavor notes: hoppy,
light-bodied lager
Main source: malt and/or
cereal
Alcohol content: 4–6%
Substitution: lager

BEER (CONTINUED)

PORTER
Flavor notes: rich, sweet, full-bodied ale
Main source: malt and/or cereal
Alcohol content: 5–6%
Substitution: stout

STOUT
Flavor notes: strong, dark, malty ale
Main source: malt and/or cereal
Alcohol content: 5–7%
Substitution: porter

WHEAT
Flavor notes: light, refreshing
Main source: wheat
Alcohol content: 4–5%
Substitution: pilsner

WHITE
Flavor notes: refreshing, slightly spicy, grapefruit
Main source: wheat
Alcohol content: 4–5%
Substitution: wheat beer and lemon

BENEDICTINE
Flavor notes: sweet herbal, citrus, medicinal, bitter
Main source: brandy
Alcohol content: 40%
Substitution: none

BENEDICTINE & BRANDY (B&B)
Flavor notes: spicy, herbal, ginger, orange
Main source: brandy
Alcohol content: 39%
Substitution: combine Benedictine, brandy and orange liqueur

BITTERS
Flavor notes: herbs, pepper
Main source: roots, herbs
Alcohol content: 40%
Substitution: none

BLUE CURACAO
Flavor notes: sweet candied orange, jammy
Main source: alcohol, orange rind
Alcohol content: 15–24%
Substitution: Cointreau, Grand Marnier, triple sec

BOURBON (SEE WHISKEY/AMERICAN)

BRANDY
Flavor notes: pronounced grape, caramel, wood
Main source: white wine
Alcohol content: 35–45%
Substitution: armagnac, cognac

BUTTERSCOTCH LIQUEUR/SCHNAPPS
Flavor notes: butterscotch, vanilla, caramel
Main source: alcohol, butterscotch
Alcohol content: 15–17%
Substitution: honey/maple liqueur

CALVADOS
Flavor notes: apple, caramel, vanilla
Main source: brandy
Alcohol content: 40–43%
Substitution: combine brandy or cognac and apple cider

CAMPARI
Flavor notes: bittersweet herbal, orange
Main source: 60 herbs, spices, fruit peel and alcohol
Alcohol content: 24.7%
Substitution: none

CAVA (SEE WINE/SPARKLING)

CHAMBORD
Flavor notes: black raspberry
Main source: cognac, raspberry, herbs
Alcohol content: 23%
Substitution: Framboise/raspberry liqueur

CHAMPAGNE (SEE WINE/SPARKLING)

CHARTREUSE
Flavor notes: bitter herb, sandalwood, cloves
Main source: wine, herbs and botanicals
Alcohol content: 55%
Substitution: none

CHERRY BRANDY/WHISKY
Flavor notes: sweet cherry pie, spice
Main source: brandy/whisky, cherries
Alcohol content: 15–24%
Substitution: combine brandy or whisky and cherry essence

CHOCOLATE CREAM LIQUEUR
Flavor notes: chocolate and/or fruit
Main source: distilled alcohol, chocolate, cream and/or fruit
Alcohol content: 12–17%
Substitution: combine Irish Cream and chocolate syrup

CIDER
Flavor notes: crisp apple, acidic
Main source: apples
Alcohol content: 5–7%
Substitution: none

CINNAMON SCHNAPPS (SEE GOLDSCHLÄGER)

COCONUT RUM (SEE RUM/COCONUT)

COFFEE CREAM LIQUEUR
Flavor notes: coffee, mocha, butterscotch
Main source: distilled alcohol, coffee, cream
Alcohol content: 15–17%
Substitution: combine Irish Cream and brewed coffee or espresso

COFFEE LIQUEUR
Flavor notes: coffee, vanilla
Main source: alcohol, coffee
Alcohol content: 20%
Substitution: Kahlúa, Tia Maria

COGNAC
Flavor notes: rich fruit, caramel, oak
Main source: white grapes
Alcohol content: 40%
Substitution: armagnac, brandy

COINTREAU
Flavor notes: bittersweet, tangy orange
Main source: brandy, orange rind
Alcohol content: 40%
Substitution: triple sec, Grand Marnier

CRÈME DE BANANE
Flavor notes: sweet banana candy, spice
Main source: alcohol, bananas
Alcohol content: 15–23%
Substitution: brandy and banana essence

CRÈME DE CACAO (WHITE AND DARK)
Flavor notes: sweet/dark cocoa, cream
Main source: alcohol, chocolate
Alcohol content: 15–24%
Substitution: chocolate cream liqueur

CRÈME DE CASSIS
Flavor notes: sweet black currant, jammy
Main source: alcohol, black currants
Alcohol content: 18–25%
Substitution: Chambord

CRÈME DE MENTHE (WHITE AND GREEN)
Flavor notes: sweet spearmint
Main source: alcohol, mint
Alcohol content: 15%
Substitution: peppermint schnapps

DRAMBUIE
Flavor notes: sweet herbs, smoky scotch, honey
Main source: scotch, honey
Alcohol content: 40%
Substitution: honey liqueur

FRAMBOISE (RASPBERRY LIQUEUR)
Flavor notes: sweet, candied raspberries
Main source: alcohol, raspberries
Alcohol content: 16%
Substitution: Chambord

FRANGELICO
Flavor notes: toasted hazelnut, cocoa, vanilla
Main source: grain alcohol, hazelnuts
Alcohol content: 24%
Substitution: walnut liqueur

GIN
Flavor notes: juniper berry, citrus, floral, herbal
Main source: wheat or rye
Alcohol content: 40%
Substitution: none

GOLDSCHLÄGER
Flavor notes: spicy, syrupy cinnamon
Main source: alcohol, cinnamon
Alcohol content: 40%
Substitution: cinnamon schnapps

GRAND MARNIER
Flavor notes: sweet orange, brandy
Main source: cognac, oranges
Alcohol content: 42%
Substitution: Cointreau, triple sec

GRAPPA
Flavor notes: dry, spicy, pungent, unaged brandy
Main source: fermented grape seeds and skins (pomace)
Alcohol: 40%
Substitution: Pernod, absinthe

HONEY LIQUEUR
Flavor notes: honey, floral and herbal tones
Main source: alcohol, honey
Alcohol content: 40%
Substitution: Drambuie

HPNOTIQ
Flavor notes: grapefruit, peach, passion fruit, cognac
Main source: cognac, vodka, fruits
Alcohol content: 17%
Substitution: Alizé Bleu

IRISH CREAM LIQUEUR
Flavor notes: sweet nutty, slightly spicy
Main source: Irish whiskey, cream
Alcohol: 17%
Substitution: none

IRISH MIST
Flavor notes: sweet florals, herbs, whiskey
Main source: whiskey, herbs
Alcohol content: 35%
Substitution: none

JÄGERMEISTER
Flavor notes: herbal, spice, citrus
Main source: alcohol, herbs
Alcohol content: 35%
Substitution: none

KAHLÚA (SEE COFFEE LIQUEUR)

KIRSCH
Flavor notes: cherries
Main source: cherries
Alcohol content: 37–45%
Substitution: cherry whiskey

LIMONCELLO DI LEVA
Flavor notes: sweet lemon
Main source: alcohol, lemons
Alcohol content: 30–35%
Substitution: combine vodka, lemon essence and sugar

LYCHEE LIQUEUR
Flavor notes: sweet lychee nut, melon
Main source: alcohol, lychees
Alcohol content: 17–24%
Substitution: none

MALIBU COCONUT RUM (SEE RUM/COCONUT)

MAPLE LIQUEUR
Flavor notes: maple, coffee, butterscotch
Main source: alcohol, maple
Alcohol content: 26%
Substitution: butterscotch liqueur

MADEIRA
Flavor notes: fruit, toffee, caramel, etc.
Main source: grapes, brandy
Alcohol content: 19–20%
Substitution: port or sherry

MELON LIQUEUR
Flavor notes: sweet honeydew melon
Main source: alcohol, melon
Alcohol content: 15–24%
Substitution: none

ORANGE BRANDY
Flavor notes: sweet orange, nutmeg, slightly medicinal
Main source: brandy, orange rind
Alcohol content: 35%
Substitution: Yukon Jack

OUZO
Flavor notes: herbal licorice, spicy
Main source: grapes, star anise, licorice, cloves, angelica root
Alcohol content: 40%
Substitution: anisette, Pernod

PEACH SCHNAPPS
Flavor notes: ripe candied peach
Main source: alcohol, peaches
Alcohol content: 15–24%
Substitution: apricot brandy

PEAR LIQUEUR
Flavor notes: pear, banana candy, slightly medicinal
Main source: alcohol, pears
Alcohol content: 30%
Substitution: Xanté Poire au Cognac

PEPPERMINT SCHNAPPS
Flavor notes: sweet peppermint candy
Main source: alcohol, peppermint
Alcohol content: 22–24%
Substitution: white crème de menthe

PERNOD
Flavor notes: sweet black licorice
Main source: alcohol, aniseed
Alcohol content: 40%
Substitution: sambuca, anisette liqueur

PIMM'S NO. 1 CUP
Flavor notes: slightly bitter citrus, herbal
Main source: gin, herbs
Alcohol content: 25%
Substitution: none

PORT
Flavor notes: sweet fruit, caramel, toffee, etc.
Main source: grapes, brandy
Alcohol content: 19–20%
Substitution: Madeira, sherry

PROSECCO (SEE WINE/SPARKLING)

RUM

RUM (AMBER, DARK)
Flavor notes: molasses, vanilla, fruit
Main source: sugar cane
Alcohol content: 40–80%
Substitution: white rum

RUM (COCONUT)
Flavor notes: sweet coconut
Main source: sugar cane, coconut
Alcohol content: 20–35%
Substitution: combine rum and coconut extract

RUM (LEMON)
Flavor notes: sweet, light lemon
Main source: sugar cane, lemon
Alcohol content: 35%
Substitution: combine rum and Limoncello Di Leva

RUM (ORANGE)
Flavor notes: sweet, light orange
Main source: sugar cane, orange
Alcohol content: 35%
Substitution: combine rum and orange liqueur

RUM (RASPBERRY)
Flavor notes: sweet, light raspberry
Main source: sugar cane, raspberry
Alcohol content: 35%
Substitution: combine rum and raspberry liqueur

RUM (VANILLA)
Flavor notes: sweet, light vanilla
Main source: sugar cane, vanilla
Alcohol content: 35%
Substitution: rum and vanilla liqueur or extract

RUM (WHITE)
Flavor notes: sweet, light, neutral
Main source: sugar cane
Alcohol content: 40%
Substitution: amber rum

RYE (SEE WHISKY/CANADIAN)

SAKE/RICE WINE
Flavor notes: subtle rice, fruit, grain, herbs
Main source: rice
Alcohol content: 13–17%
Substitution: none

SAMBUCA
Flavor note: black licorice, anise, sweet
Main source: witch elder bush, licorice, sugar, herbs, spices
Alcohol content: 38%
Substitutions: ouzo, anisette

SCOTCH (SEE WHISKY/SCOTCH)

SEKT (SEE WINE/SPARKLING)

SHERRY
Flavor notes: raisins, caramel, fig, almonds
Main source: grapes, brandy
Alcohol content: 19–20%
Substitution: Port, Madeira

SLOE GIN
Flavor notes: mandarin, sloe berry
Main source: alcohol, sloe berries
Alcohol content: 15%
Substitution: none

SOUR LIQUEURS (APPLE, MELON, RASPBERRY, TANGERINE)
Flavor notes: sour, bitter fruit candy
Main source: alcohol, fruit
Alcohol content: 15%
Substitution: none

SOUTHERN COMFORT
Flavor notes: sweet peach/apricot, whiskey
Main source: whiskey, fruit
Alcohol content: 35%
Substitution: combine whiskey and peach juice

SPARKLING WINE (SEE WINE/SPARKLING)

STRAWBERRY LIQUEUR
Flavor notes: strawberry jam
Main source: alcohol, strawberries
Alcohol content: 20%
Substitution: Chambord, raspberry liqueur

TEQUILA
Flavor notes: herbal, pepper, citrus, vanilla, caramel
Main source: blue agave
Alcohol content: 40-50%
Substitution: none

TEQUILA CREAM LIQUEUR
Flavor notes: strawberry, vanilla, tequila
Main source: tequila, strawberries, cream
Alcohol content: 15%
Substitution: none

TIA MARIA (SEE COFFEE LIQUEUR)

TOFFEE CREAM LIQUEUR
Flavor notes: toffee, butterscotch, cream
Main source: distilled alcohol, toffee
Alcohol content: 17%
Substitution: Irish Cream and butterscotch syrup

TRIPLE SEC
Flavor notes: sweet, tangy orange
Main source: alcohol, orange rind
Alcohol content: 22–35%
Substitution: Cointreau, Grand Marnier

VANILLA LIQUEUR/SCHNAPPS
Flavor notes: sweet vanilla, marshmallow
Main source: alcohol, flavorings
Alcohol content: 24%
Substitution: none

VERMOUTH (DRY/WHITE)
Flavor notes: herbal, citrus, bitter
Main source: wine and brandy, herbs
Alcohol content: 18%
Substitution: white wine

VERMOUTH (SWEET/RED)
Flavor notes: bittersweet, citrus, spice
Main source: wine and brandy, herbs
Alcohol content: 16–17%
Substitution: red wine

VODKA
VODKA
Flavor notes: light herbal
Main source: grain or corn or potatoes
Alcohol content: 40–50%
Substitution: gin (in some cases)

VODKA (BERRY, STRAWBERRY)
Flavor notes: light berry, strawberry
Main source: grain, berry
Alcohol content: 35–40%
Substitution: combine vodka and berry liqueur

VODKA (BLACK CURRANT)
Flavor notes: light black currant
Main source: grain, black currants
Alcohol content: 40%
Substitution: combine vodka and cassis

VODKA (CRANBERRY)
Flavor notes: light cranberry
Main source: grain, cranberry
Alcohol content: 38%
Substitution: combine vodka and cranberry juice

VODKA (GRAPEFRUIT)
Flavor notes: light grapefruit
Main source: grain, grapefruit
Alcohol content: 38%
Substitution: combine vodka and grapefruit juice

VODKA (GREEN APPLE)
Flavor notes: light tart apple
Main source: grain, apple
Alcohol content: 35–40%
Substitution: combine vodka and apple juice

VODKA (LEMON)
Flavor notes: light lemon
Main source: grain, lemon
Alcohol content: 35–40%
Substitution: combine vodka and Limoncello Di Leva

VODKA (LIME)
Flavor notes: light lime
Main source: grain, lime
Alcohol content: 35–40%
Substitution: combine vodka and fresh lime juice or cordial

VODKA (CONTINUED)

VODKA (MANGO)
Flavor notes: light mango
Main source: grain, mango
Alcohol content: 40%
Substitution: combine vodka and mango purée

VODKA (MELON)
Flavor notes: light melon
Main source: grain, melon
Alcohol content: 23–35%
Substitution: combine vodka and melon liqueur

VODKA (ORANGE)
Flavor notes: light orange
Main source: grain, orange
Alcohol content: 40%
Substitution: combine vodka and orange liqueur

VODKA (PEACH)
Flavor notes: light peach
Main source: grain, peach
Alcohol content: 40%
Substitution: combine vodka and peach schnapps

VODKA (PEPPER)
Flavor notes: pepper
Main source: grain, pepper
Alcohol content: 40%
Substitution: combine vodka and hot sauce

VODKA (RASPBERRY)
Flavor notes: light raspberry
Main source: grain, raspberry
Alcohol content: 35–40%
Substitution: combine vodka and raspberry liqueur

VODKA (VANILLA)
Flavor notes: light vanilla
Main source: grain, vanilla
Alcohol content: 35–40%
Substitution: combine vodka and vanilla liqueur/extract

WALNUT LIQUEUR
Flavor notes: toasted walnut
Main source: grain alcohol, walnuts
Alcohol content: 24%
Substitution: Frangelico

WHISKEY

WHISKEY (AMERICAN/BOURBON)
Flavor notes: smoke, caramel, floral, spice
Main source: corn and other grain(s)
Alcohol content: 40–75%
Substitution: rye, scotch, Irish whiskey

WHISKEY (IRISH)
Flavor notes: smoke, fruit, butter, oak
Main source: barley or wheat or corn
Alcohol content: 40%
Substitution: bourbon, rye, scotch

WHISKY (CANADIAN/RYE)
Flavor notes: grain, vanilla, toffee etc.
Main source: rye
Alcohol content: 40%
Substitution: bourbon, scotch, Irish whiskey

WHISKY (SCOTCH—BLENDED AND SINGLE MALT)
Flavor notes: caramel, honey, herbs, floral, spice, smoke, peat
Main source: barley or wheat or corn
Alcohol content: 40–75%
Substitution: bourbon, rye, Irish whiskey

WINE

WINE (DESSERT)
Flavor notes: sweet, intense fruit, acidic
Main source: grapes (red or white)
Alcohol content: 10–14%
Substitution: late harvest Riesling, late harvest Vidal

WINE (ICE)
Flavor notes: sweet, intense fruit, acidic
Main source: frozen grapes (red or white)
Alcohol content: 10–14%
Substitution: late harvest Riesling, Vidal, dessert wine

WINE (RED)
Flavor notes: various
Main source: red grapes
Alcohol content: 8–17%
Substitution: sweet vermouth, port (in small amounts)

WINE (ROSÉ)
Flavor notes: various
Main source: red and/or white grapes
Alcohol content: 8–17%
Substitution: dry vermouth, sherry (in small amounts)

WINE (SPARKLING)
Flavor notes: various
Main source: red and/or white grapes
Alcohol content: 8–17%
Substitution: cava, champagne, prosecco, sekt

WINE (WHITE)
Flavor notes: various
Main source: white grapes
Alcohol content: 8–17%
Substitution: dry vermouth, sherry (in small amounts)

XANTÉ POIRE AU COGNAC
Flavor notes: sweet, jammy pear
Main source: cognac, pears
Alcohol content: 38%
Substitution: pear liqueur

YUKON JACK
Flavor notes: sweet orange rind, whisky
Main source: whisky, orange rind
Alcohol content: 40%
Substitution: orange brandy

Index

COOKING WITH BOOZE

COOKING WITH BOOZE

CHEERS!

Writing a book turns out to be a lot of work—more than either of us imagined—possible only with a team of amazing people around us.

Thanks to our friends at Whitecap: Robert for believing we could pull this off, Leslie for editing the hell out of us (in all the right ways) and AnnMarie for keeping us on track.

Thanks to Geoffrey and Jeff for your visual talents. Without you guys this book would be just a bunch of words. Your contribution is paramount.

Big thanks to Five for turning our words and Geoffrey's pictures into something tangible—and fantastic looking, by the way. And thanks to Devon for shooting our mugs for the back of this book. You managed to make us look better than we do in person and for that reason alone, we love you.

Special thanks to Yaman and the rest of Those Drunk Guys—Gord, Jamie, Dennis, Mirwin and McKizzo—for being our kitchen guinea pigs and who were always around to raise a pint when we needed to.

Thank you to all of our friends and families for their support and love and for bragging about us to anyone who'd listen. We couldn't ask for better promotion.

Finally, a huge thanks to HomeSense for providing all of the props for photography. Thanks to Plymouth gin, Cruzan rum and Berringer wines for your generous donations and to Sherri at Courtney Rainey Group and Angela at Foster's Wine Estates for making it happen.

Visit www.CookingWithBooze.com
for more recipes and tips.